ANSWERS FROM THE AFTERLIFE

Answers from the Afterlife

And Spiritual Reflections

Prudence Ann Smith MD

Copyright © 2016 Prudence Ann Smith MD
All rights reserved.

ISBN: 069280434X
ISBN 13: 9780692804346
Library of Congress Control Number: 2016918307
Belle Publishers, Tulare, CALIFORNIA

Dedicated to
My loved one and guide in spirit —
How can I ever thank you enough
for being you and loving me?
Also with gratitude to my guides, Harvey's guides,
and the other souls who have shared the journey with me.

The world is too small without you
Since we had to part,
Contentment now escapes me
And joy evades my heart,
For you are the living poem,
The soul within my song,
Without you the words are empty
The melody is wrong,

I thank you for your love
And for being you,
For standing by me through the storm,
Your love forever true,
For love is long and time is short -
A promise do I keep,
And when you hold me close again,
No more will I weep.

FORWARD

This book is an upbeat, intellectual odyssey, an exploration of the ultimate questions we ask about ourselves and the universe, in essence, spiritual detective work.

It bridges the categories of gender and age to include all those on a spiritual quest and is written for the everyday explorer, the intellectual seeker, the applied philosopher, those who seek to answer the "whys" of life, those who seek to understand life from a spiritual, mystical, non-physical perspective, those who have experienced loss and grief, those who question their purpose or destiny, those who are interested in other dimensions and realities – the supernatural, paranormal world, those who think outside the box, those interested in channeling and mediumship, and those with inquiries about spiritual gifts and second sight.

What this book is about

Who doesn't like a good mystery? The greatest mystery is the one that surrounds us – our world. While modern scientists such as Stephen Hawking try to unravel the physical mysteries of our universe, this book explores the spiritual mysteries.

PRUDENCE ANN SMITH MD

Trained in the scientific discipline of medicine, but coming from a family with a medium for a grandmother, Dr. Smith brings a unique perspective to the biggest and most compelling questions of life – and the result is a blend of logical analysis and communication with those who know best, those who are there – the dead.

The first part of the book is a series of questions with answers channeled by two mediums from their afterlife guides. The second portion includes intriguing questions examined and analyzed from the perspectives of personal experience, literary research, and logical analysis.

The book addresses questions such as these: Why are we here? What is the soul? Do we all have lessons to learn? Do we each have a mission in life? Do we live multiple lives? Can we know the future? Do our guides give us warnings? Is there a clear-cut right and wrong? Why are some people negative? How can we end negative cycles in our lives? How do we forgive those who have hurt us? How do predestination and free will affect us? Are events in our lives pre-planned? Can knowing about a past life help us? Is there a formula for finding happiness? Why do different mediums sometimes give conflicting messages? Are there evil spirits? Do we have a soul group? What do our guides do? Are there eternal records of our lives - our thoughts, deeds, and words? Can those who have passed on still be with us? How do we change when we die? If we all have souls with divine origin, why did God create us? Where did God come from – what is the origin of existence? How do spirits look, communicate, and live? Do we get a second chance and live again? Is there justice and what is karma? Is love eternal? What happens to all the conflicting religions and ideologies when we get to the other side? What kind of afterlife does each of us go to? What are heaven and hell? Is it possible to not know you're dead? What are the many mansions described in religious texts? Is there such a thing as enlightenment? What is our ultimate destiny?

This book chronicles one doctor's spiritual odyssey, the personal journey of a "spiritual detective" on the ultimate quest to unravel the secrets of the universe, to explore answers to the deepest questions of mankind's existence, the riddles that have intrigued us from time immemorial.

TABLE OF CONTENTS

Forward · ix

Part I
Answers from the Afterlife

Never Too Old · 3
Personal Identity and Purpose · · · · · · · · · · · · · · · · · · 4
Encounters of the Best Kind · · · · · · · · · · · · · · · · · · · 6
How It All Started · 26
The Soul · 32
Recognizing and Dealing with Negative Influences · · · · · · · · · · 33
Negative Communication · 37
Past Life Relationships · 39
Absolute Truth · 41
People from Prior Lifetimes · · · · · · · · · · · · · · · · · · 42
Spiritual Lessons · 44
Reliving Lessons · 45
Spirits and Euphoria · 47
Spirit Sightings · 48
Memories of Prior Lives · 49
Are Spirits Ever Annihilated? · · · · · · · · · · · · · · · · 51
Do We Remember Earth Lives? · · · · · · · · · · · · · · 52

Mediumship Readings of the Living · · · · · · · · · · · · · · 53
OBE's and Foreknowledge of Death · · · · · · · · · · · · · 54
Clarity of Mediumship Communication · · · · · · · · · · · · 56
Advice/Warnings from Guides · · · · · · · · · · · · · · · · 57
Meeting Our Guides in the Afterlife · · · · · · · · · · · · · · 58
Spiritual Values ·60
Precognition ·61
Reincarnation ·62
Forgiveness and Moving On · · · · · · · · · · · · · · · · · · ·63
Spirit Appearance ·64
Moral Values ·66
NDE's and Predestination ·67
Non-Human Spirits ·69
Consensus on Right and Wrong · · · · · · · · · · · · · · · ·71
Life Review · 72
Divided Souls ·73
Purpose ·75
Animal Spirits ·76
Akashic Records · 77
Happy Incarnations ·78
Relevancy of Right and Wrong · · · · · · · · · · · · · · · · ·79
Spirit Communication ·81
Guides ·84
Soul Group ·86
Déjà vu ·87
Conflicting Messages ·88
Feelings of Euphoria ·89
Different Answers ·92
Information from Past Lives · · · · · · · · · · · · · · · · · · ·93
Pre-Planning Traumatic Events · · · · · · · · · · · · · · · · ·95

Evil Spirits ·96
Inspiration ·98
Advice ·99
Relationship with Guides ·100
Human Cruelty ·101
Negative Personalities ·102
Aligning Karma ·103
Karma and Punishment ·104
Relationships in the Afterlife ·105
Wise Advice ·106
Inspirational Advice ·107
Warnings from Guides ·108
Divine Purpose ·111
Divine Purpose and Free Will ·112
Creation of Souls ·113
Origin of God ·115
The Nature of God ·117

Part II
Reflections on Spirit

Who Says Understanding Is Easy? · · · · · · · · · · · · · · · ·121
Communicating with Spirit ·126
The Service of Mediumship ·128
Charmed Lives? ·130
Empaths, Sensitives, and Peculiar Views of the Afterlife · · · · · ·131
Souls Who Act in Good or Evil · · · · · · · · · · · · · · · · · ·135
What Is the Truth? Negative and Positive Souls · · · · · · · · · · · ·139
Retention of Identity ·145
Spirit Senses ·148

Spirit Appearance ·152
Planning Reincarnations ·155
Planning Our Lives ·157
Negativity and Positivity ·160
Ending Negative Relationships · · · · · · · · · · · · · · · · · ·164
Fear of Loss ·166
Free Will and Guidance ·168
Help in Moving On ·170
Ending Negative Cycles ·173
Abuse, healing, and forgiveness · · · · · · · · · · · · · · · · · ·175
Releasing the Fetters ·177
Discarding Emotional Baggage, Making Better Choices · · · · · ·179
Purpose and Progress ·183
Karma ·187
Transparency ·190
Trust and service ·192
Commitment ·194
Personal and Humanitarian Love · · · · · · · · · · · · · · · · ·195
Lasting Love ·201
Unions ·204
Merging and Sex ·208
Twin Flames ·210
Levels ·211
Recalling Past Experience ·212
Finding My Own Truth ·213
Different Realities ·216
Your Own Journey- Choices in the Afterlife · · · · · · · · · · · ·219
Conflicting Viewpoints ·223
Creating Your World ·225
Creators ·227

The Place of Dreams Come True · · · · · · · · · · · · · · · · · 228
A Place of Unconditional Love · · · · · · · · · · · · · · · · · · 230
Ideologies · 231
Soul Groups · 232
Reincarnation · 233
Purpose · 235
Enlightenment · 237
Ultimate Destiny · 238

Part III
Observation and Speculation

Shared Human/Spirit Mental Experiences · · · · · · · · · · · · · · · 241
Are Souls Happier in the Afterlife or on Earth? · · · · · · · · · · · · 244
What Accounts for Personality Changes in People? · · · · · · · · · 245
Why Do Some Souls Have Worse Tempers? · · · · · · · · · · · · · · 248
Why Do People Act with Cruelty? · 249
What about Justice, Breaking the Law, and
Capital Punishment? · 250
Demons? No Demons? Going, 1,2,3. · · · · · · · · · · · · · · · · · 252
Time Travel – Past and Future · 256
Truth and Imperfect People, Imperfect Mediums · · · · · · · · · · 259
Lessons, Justice, and Purpose · 267
Negative Baggage, Spiders' Webs · 271
Learning Lessons Together · 273
The Many Mansions of the Afterlife · · · · · · · · · · · · · · · · · · 276
Do We Instantly Forgive and Heal when We Die? · · · · · · · · · · 278
Personal Love · 282
The Afterlife and Quantum Physics · · · · · · · · · · · · · · · · · · · 287
Simultaneous Lives, Time, Timelessness, and Learning · · · · · · 288

Inconsistencies of the Multiple Simultaneous
Reincarnational Selves Theory ·······················290
Dead or Alive······································293
How Soon Is Too Soon?·····························295
Conclusions ······································298
Personal Love – A Final Thought·····················305
The Final Assessment······························306
The Finishing Touch ·······························308

Postscript···309
Bibliography······································315
About the Author ·································319

PART I

ANSWERS FROM THE AFTERLIFE

This section contains a series of questions asked by a colleague, Harvey, and myself of our guides. Each is dated and answers were channeled.

Never Too Old

I recently had the privilege of meeting a 105 year old lady who still hosts spiritual group meetings in her home. A friend and I chatted with her for several hours and gave her and her friend readings. The spirits from the other side were very eager to come through and I brought through her best friend, the other lady's husband, and an in-law who had died in a war and received a Purple Heart.

After the readings, our host described how her two former husbands had recently appeared at the foot of her bed. When she spoke to them they vanished. I explained to her that it takes a lot of energy for spirits to manifest themselves and most who can only appear momentarily. She felt that they were there to let her know she had their support and I feel their visit may have been in honor of her recent birthday.

I was inspired to tell her that I felt she had abilities as a medium and was prompted by Spirit to ask her to give me a brief reading. She brought through my loved one in Spirit, describing him and giving me a simple message from him, which was totally characteristic of what he would have said. I was astounded and delighted. Here was a 105 year old lady giving her first reading and it was valid and accurate. I learned something that day. You are never too old to connect with Spirit or learn something new.

PERSONAL IDENTITY AND PURPOSE

I read an article today that reminded me of how unique each one of us is. Of course we all need clothing, food, shelter, jobs, education, etc. and we want to be happy, successful and fulfilled, but that means something different for each of us.

Whenever I hear a medium say that we lose our personalities, opinions, and individual identities - all the things that make us who we are- on the other side, I think hogwash. What's left if our personalities and identities are annihilated and if the person I call me is gone? Why exist in the first place? If I am no longer me, all the things I've done or cared about are irrelevant.

The article I read was written by a writer assessing his life and what he had learned. He summed it up as "nothing means anything" and the only constant in his life is that he bounces back from disappointments and problems quicker.

I couldn't be any more different from him. I'm happy to say everything means something to me, good or bad. Some things mean so much to me that I can't imagine living without them- like the relationships I have with those I love, like the opportunities to try to do something good or positive with the time and life I have, and like my faith that there is a supreme being and a purpose in our lives.

I am also glad I have others that I am close to both in the spirit world and on the earth who, like me, love someone, find meaning in life, and have goals and accomplishments near to their heart. I am convinced we remain individuals on the other side with our personalities intact and if I have any choice in the matter you will find me with a group of passionate loving individuals who seek spiritual truth, find meaning in love, cherish those dear to them, know happiness, and are making efforts to become better people.

ENCOUNTERS OF THE BEST KIND

The blending

I was enchanted and delighted at our last Spirit circle by a wonderful medium whom I will refer to as K who also happens to be a wonderful person. She is around 90 years of age and a former schoolteacher. She was giving a message to another excellent medium, E, who is also a channeler, when E's father came through. The father is a very strong spirit who was concerned about his daughter's inattention when she was getting calls while driving and for her haste in getting from one place to another. We saw little K, a sweet, soft-spoken, gentle older lady, turn into a very vocal, annoyed, and worried "papa bear", concerned for his daughter. K was a completely different person, getting louder and really letting the other medium have it. Because that was so unlike K, it was funny to see, and we all started laughing, which perturbed her Dad's spirit even more, and little K put her hand on her hip and very sternly reprimanded us all— "I'm serious. You're laughing. This isn't funny." And he addressed his daughter, "You have a purpose here yet. I don't want you to be driving incautiously. Pay attention!"

With that the message was over, and quiet, demure, little K came back. Laughing, she said, "He invaded me." It was so humorous to see her, a gentle, quiet soul, turn into an aggressive man. K is a "sleeper". She is a very sweet, kind lady with an almost shy demeanor and it's funny to see her become someone totally uncharacteristic of her. She's given me a similar reading before and it's a real gift to see her transform into your loved one, with mannerisms, speech patterns, and the personality of your loved one, right before your eyes. When my loved one came through her once, he said, "I want to put my arms around you and kiss you, Penny." That message meant a lot to me.

A lesson from the afterlife

It was a privilege to work with a very talented medium as three of us gave a message to a guest sitter. The sitter had experienced a difficult situation in her life involving the spirit who was coming through. The Spirit came through together with her husband, holding hands with him. It was conveyed that they were very close and happy to be together, still a couple. She came through to say she was sorry for something she had done while alive and comfort the sitter, who was in tears. Another medium gave the main part of the reading, but I got the message that we all see the bigger picture when we go across and learn how we affected other people by our actions and choices. When we have caused harm we feel what the other person felt and need to make things right, to make amends for the well-being of both ourselves and the other person before we can move forward and be free of guilt.

At the end of the reading I saw another spirit come up from behind and put his arms on each of their shoulders, standing in the middle behind them. They were a couple in a second marriage and he had been married to the male spirit's first wife. They were friendly, with no hard feelings, helping each other. I remembered how, while he was alive, after telling his wife what he had learned from each of his prior relationships, he had asked his wife-to-be what he was going to learn from her and, although she didn't say it out loud, she had thought, "From me you are going to learn love." And he did. He stays by her from the Spirit world, helping and comforting her. But in this case he demonstrated love toward his former wife's first husband and his second wife. There was no malice. He was there supporting them, friendly as could be, the typical gallant, outgoing soul he was in life. He was demonstrating the love his wife had said he was going to learn from her when they were courting.

When I asked him, he told me, "We appreciate one another. We assist each other." So there was one of my questions answered. Spirit has a way of doing that. If you need understanding or insight into some concept, they'll answer you in words, but also show you with their behavior.

I'm always thankful for these explanations.

I remember when my friend, Harvey, and I first went to his house and he was still there in spirit. We could hear him and feel his personality so strongly. If you asked me if I knew him I would say yes just as surely as if we had been good friends for a long time. It's funny because we never met him in life, but we feel as though we know him just the same. Whenever we went to visit his wife, we felt his presence in the home, warm and welcoming, a proud host happy to have us there.

One thing I learned from this is that Spirit cares for us despite our faults, knowing that they had faults, too. They try to help us navigate the rough waters of life and give us help with truths they learned from their own lives.

Answers from the Afterlife

Having fun

At our last Spirit circle a group of us who were old friends and had each lost someone very dear to us got seated together to give readings. We each were going through a difficult patch in our lives and every one of those loved ones came through with a resounding message. The other side doesn't lack humor and they didn't disappoint.

Each spirit came through with their characteristic personality, making us laugh until we were practically hysterical. We couldn't stop laughing. Each spirit came through dressed up dramatically and exhibiting their characteristics in a funny and candid way. As we laughed more and more, the energy kept getting higher and we kept getting warmer. Each spirit came through pulling out all the stops, not to be outdone by the one who came before him. The specific information was astounding but the way the personality of each spirit came through was even better. My loved one was there "with bells on". Just like in a friendly group people "let their hair down" and reveal their character, in our little friendly group the spirits did the same. My loved one had me and the others in stitches. He was showing his personality and how phenomenally he looked and dressed and the medium accurately described how I physically feel his energy. The medium giving me the message also picked up on how I looked when we were together and his response to something we had been discussing the night before. I was wiping my forehead and almost left speechless at the humor and intensity of the messages. I saw one spirit giving his mother a beautifully wrapped box with pink paper and ribbon and the "sleeper", K, said there was a pearl in the box, which the mother confirmed her son had given her in a pink wrapped box just before he passed.

Even though we couldn't see our loved ones with our physical eyes, we were communicating with them just like a group of intimate friends. For that one evening, the "perceived" wall between the worlds disappeared.

Thanksgiving Dinner

I was recently at a Spirit circle just before Thanksgiving where a dad in spirit came through to his daughter. E's dad has quite a personality and is very funny. After complimenting her that her driving has become much better since he gave her a scolding at a previous Spirit circle, he started to reminisce about the food he loved so much. He wanted her to make sweet Kugle, with sugar, cinnamon, raisins, and noodles. That started the ball rolling and each subsequent spirit that came through longed for their favorite dish. I know that spirits still think about food even though they don't have the kind of bodies that require food. One spirit even told her granddaughter not to go to Marie Callender's, but to cook instead, leave a chair open, and she would show up for the celebration.

That started me thinking. I know my loved one can hear what I'm thinking and feel exactly what I'm feeling. Since the physical sensations, including taste, are processed in the brain, he must be able to taste what I'm eating, smell what I'm smelling, and hear what I'm hearing. He had already come through at Spirit circles to say he enjoyed the songs I wrote and played for him. Several other mediums at the circle substantiated this from their experiences. I have to admit that now when I go to a restaurant, sometimes I order something I know my loved one liked, just for him, and we enjoy it together. But no liver. He's out of luck if he wants that one. But, seriously, I am thrilled that we can still enjoy all those things together. Since spirits come through to say they appreciate a tribute one of their loved ones organized for them, or loved the fact that a loved one got a tattoo in their honor, why not a song, a poem, a special celebration or a favorite dish? I think I'd better get the recipe book out and hone my cooking skills!

Special Delivery

At that same Spirit circle a dear friend of mine, D, a mother who had lost a son, was thrilled when her son came through, giving me all sorts of specific personal information, but not letting me recognize who he was. Each piece of information that came through, the mountain climbing, the olive colored jacket, the Tom Cruise reference, the love of sports, the sensitive side, the military/American flag connection, the red balloon she sent up in his honor, were all corroborated. Another medium saw her writing letters to him and then a third medium said, why is E's dad delivering the letters to D's son? E spoke up and said, "My dad was a mail carrier in life." Wow, spirit had a wonderful sense of humor to say that D's son was getting the letters she wrote to him delivered to him by E's dad, who was a mail carrier, now in spirit.

All of a sudden the sometimes serious, proper nature of some spirit circles dissolves and turns into this wonderful, fun-loving intimate gathering of loved ones and friends, both "dead" and alive, having a great time together, laughing, just as they had in life. It is so natural compared to the regimented messages given by some mediums who give good evidence of survival, but sometimes fail to capture the essence of the person. That one night our loved ones were there sitting next to us, free to be the same kooky, endearing, loving, individuals they were in life — not cardboard cutouts only allowed to give names, ranks, and serial numbers, but instead real three-dimensional people "so to speak", the same people we loved and lost, except now they were no longer lost. They were right there with us being themselves. And that was better evidence than anything else. More treasured and coveted communication, the chance to love and embrace them with our hearts as we had done in life. It doesn't get any better than that.

My dog, the medium

Can a dog be a medium? That question never crossed my mind until yesterday. We had a small Skype spirit circle and all of a sudden one of the mediums said, " I have a dog coming through. It's wearing a fluffy pink decoration around its neck and it has jumped up on me three times. It's mostly black, medium sized, and it is showing me its tongue hanging down out of the corner of its mouth. I'm getting that something went wrong with the digestive system. I'm hearing Christmas music, the song 'Here comes Santa Claus — here comes Santa Claus right down Santa Claus Lane.' The dog is inside a Christmas box. It keeps pushing things around with its nose. It's drinking something other than water out of your cup." With that, the medium's dog, Charlie, did something it had never done before. It jumped up with its paws on her chest, looking down on her, straight into her eyes, and just stood there. K, the medium, was surprised and said, "Charlie's channeling your dog. He's never done this before. The dog is making me feel it's happy and has companionship. It's not alone. It's saying, 'I'm with the others.'" The statement was appropriate, as I had lost three dogs in my lifetime before Angel passed. I look forward to seeing her and the others on "The Rainbow Bridge".

I couldn't believe the reading. My dog, Angel, was a medium-sized, mostly black beagle. All of my dogs had Christmas names, Angel, Holly, Jingles, Belle, Dancer, and Noel. One was even a Christmas present. I have a picture of Angel with Santa Claus taken by the ASPCA at Christmas with her wearing a fluffy pink wreath around her neck. She was the most forward of the dogs, always jumping up on me and her most characteristic position was standing with her paws on my chest looking down at me, just like Charlie did to the medium. I think she showed herself pushing things around because she was "pushy"- the most forward of my dogs. She liked to drink tea with milk out of my teacup whenever she could get hold of it. And she used to get a few sips of milkshake from my cup whenever I had one. She died with a digestive problem – aspiration - and her tongue was hanging out of the side of her mouth in the final moments. I was hoping she would be with her predecessors, Jingles, Belle, and Holly, who had crossed over before Angel. Every detail was correct. I was beyond thrilled to hear from her, to know she was okay and not alone. But what shocked me the most was the fact that Charlie, the medium's dog, assumed Angel's most characteristic pose, which was something he had never done before. Imagine that – a dog, a medium.

My dog, Angel, who came through, is pictured below.

Answers from the Afterlife

Seeking spiritual truth

Some of the answers I have received in this book appear to be simple, or truisms. But sometimes when someone is puzzled or perplexed about situations in their life, as the old adage goes, they "can't see the forest for the trees." What are the most important words I have ever heard? "I love you." How many times has that been said and how simple is that? Yet that is the most important thing to me. Sometimes the most important realizations are the simplest. Something doesn't have to be esoteric or arcane to be the truth.

Spiritual truths are not hidden. God doesn't play games with us. The most important principles and truths are available to every human being, but sometimes we can't see them. They are really a part of our soul, our inner wisdom and knowledge, but become distorted by the circumstances of our lives, the experiences we have on earth.

I recall one teaching seminar I attended with the medium, A. J. Barrera. He gave us an exercise in which we were given pictures of famous people in sealed envelopes and instructed to get information psychically about the individual as we held the sealed envelope. I won't give the name of the celebrity that was in my envelope as these celebrities were deceased and not here to defend themselves, but I got a clear image of this famous person, not physically, but spiritually, and I saw a mirror distorting his perception of life. When I later found out who this person was, I felt the image I got was highly appropriate. I mention this because it illustrates how our understanding of the events we're going through can become clouded or unclear. I do believe we have answers to most of the important questions within us, just disguised and hidden by the confusion of life events and self doubt.

We can often be influenced by the behavior of others and take that to be correct when it isn't. For a number of years I became cynical because of how some other people had treated me and began to think their callous, uncaring, selfish behavior was right and I was wrong. Certainly there must be something wrong with me, not them. After all, they had money, power, and privilege; they could do what they wanted without seeming repercussions. They must be right. But they stepped on people and used people. They lied and harmed others. I became brainwashed to an extent – poisoned by them to accept that their way of thinking was right because it seemed to be rewarded in the physical world.

But there's the word – physical. In the physical world they had what seemed like good fortune – good jobs, security, money, respect from the community, and they seemed to be right no matter what they did. In other words, they had a picture perfect life on the surface. But one day an African American female doctor in the Bronx, who was an attending teaching me as a resident, gave me a lesson in more than medicine. She described how she had a mother with a mental disorder who was institutionalized and how she and her brothers practically raised themselves in poverty with some help from an overburdened father. She had to fight every step of the way to rise above her circumstances and became a successful doctor. But what she said next was the most memorable. She said when people mistreat you, you are not wrong, you do not deserve that, they are wrong. You must respect yourself and not be influenced by them to lose your convictions and start to think or behave like them. You must not justify wrong by seeing that in the world wrong is often rewarded.

That day changed my mind. Instead of feeling that those who had exploited me must be correct because they seemed to have been rewarded by "God" because they had good things in their lives, I now saw that they were rewarded in the material world, not the spiritual world, and that, in effect, they were "dry bones" in "whited sepulchers." The truth isn't always what you see around you. It is what you know in you, freely given, but you must recognize it, because within all the clamor and cacophony of the world with all its gaudy distractions, sometimes the truth is a "still, small voice."

When I was a student in college, I took comparative religion because I was a seeker, always seeking after the truth of life, the meaning of life. Although I later became involved with a particular religion, I do not believe that any one religion or sect has the exclusive truth or the exclusive favor of God. When I discuss spiritual principles with someone of a different religion, I always say that it is not the person, the historical circumstances described in any religious text that are important. It is the principles set forth, the moral values that help us to interact with other people, that help us to lead productive lives, that are important. Truths, I believe, are universal. The individual cultural values, mores, and folkways of an individual culture, society, or nation may vary, and do on the earth. But it is the deeper, larger spiritual principles that are more important, that are at the heart of our progress as souls.

How do we not judge others?

When I ask myself how can I not judge others who are obviously doing wrong, stealing, lying, cheating, exploiting, oppressing, murdering, controlling, or abusing others, the only answer I come up with is that they are learning lessons like me. Perhaps that is their lesson, the one they haven't learned yet. Do I wish to be condemned for things I did wrong out of ignorance, out of unawareness? One spirit coming through in a spirit circle told me there is a difference between being "evil" and being unaware, uninformed.

I can understand that and realize that if we were perfect already, we wouldn't need to be here learning lessons. Do we blame someone for something they don't know or can't understand at the time? I can understand others undergoing similar trials as I myself have done things I wish I hadn't done out of ignorance. Picture a little child in a sandbox having a quarrel with another child. That's how we must look at times.

But what about the case in which someone deliberately harms another, enjoys causing pain, rapes, murderers, tortures and kills? How are we capable of not judging such actions when we ourselves may be the victims of such deeds, when our families may be involved? I think perhaps the crux of the matter is in the phrase "judging such actions", rather than judging such people. In the Bible, it's stated that we should not hate the person, but hate the deed or action. I think it is particularly difficult to understand or forgive heinous behavior, particularly when we or our loved ones are the victims.

But I have heard of situations in which people were able to look beyond their circumstances and forgive someone who has committed an unthinkable crime, rather than seeking retribution, matching "an eye for an eye," but instead maintaining their own dignity and not sinking to the level of the person who committed the crime. I admire such people, who are strong enough to abide by their own values, to preserve decorum in the face of atrocities.

Maybe there is a greater purpose difficult to see when we are in the thick of the battle. I guess in order to understand we must see both sides of the coin, be both the oppressed and the oppressor, the victim and the perpetrator, at different times in order to understand fully our own actions and the actions of others, the spiritual repercussions of our decisions and behavior. If we are never the victim, how can we understand the effects of wrongdoing? If we are never the oppressor, how can we ever understand the effects of our wrongdoing upon others? As one medium and psychic detective put it, if we never understand hate, how can we understand love? We can only fully understand what we have experienced personally. But to understand the difference between right and wrong, love and hate, kindness and cruelty, we must experience both, and I believe that is why we are here in a world with choices, with free will, with negativity and positivity.

How we cannot judge someone who has tortured and killed a loved one, I don't know. Certainly we judge the acts, but perhaps there is a time when we become spiritual enough to be able to forgive the soul. I think of Jesus on the cross saying, regarding his killers, "Forgive them, they know not what they do." Perhaps we come to a point in our spiritual evolution when we are able to do that. I do not claim to be at that point. But I do understand the principle. I guess it is a matter of strength and spiritual fortitude, enlightenment, and advancement.

I do not take this to mean that we are to passively accept abuse, violence against us, or deliberate harm. I do believe we have the right to defend ourselves as well as the obligation to defend ourselves and our loved ones from deliberate harm. When we are in an abusive situation we must either have the strength to get out of it or the strength to tolerate or live with it. Both choices will have repercussions.

PRUDENCE ANN SMITH MD

Do I believe in punishment? Yes, in the regard that if there are no repercussions or consequences for our actions, we never learn to cease repeating the same deeds and mistakes. However, I also believe that that is what karma is for. The Bible says "vengeance is mine". In other words, retribution is not the answer, but protecting ourselves from the violence of others is important. Although sometimes we may wish that others might experience, themselves, the harm that they caused us, sometimes it seems that they do. I have been involved in several situations in which the unfair and detrimental deeds of others came back upon them and they suffered a sort of justice that I would not have expected. I can't say that I enjoyed seeing people suffer the consequences of their own behavior, but in a way felt vindicated, thinking that the person who treated me so badly might not do that to others or harm others anymore.

Forgiveness? As far as forgiveness, I have forgiven everyone in my life who has caused me pain or harmed me. I do not hold any malice against any of them. I only seek to be freed from situations in which I am currently oppressed or harmed. It is difficult to cope with anger when you are being abused in real time. Perhaps it is someone who is verbally demeaning and abusive, who enjoys attempting to erode your self-respect and self-esteem by cursing, shouting, and deprecating you. That kind of person is usually unwilling to discuss anything rationally or to change their behavior. Usually that type of person feels they are always right and have done no wrong. I believe that those of us who have undergone such misuse have done so because it is part of our path to learn how to cope with such difficult situations either by suffering the consequences of withdrawing from the situation or by standing up to the abuser.

When people do wrong, there is often no perfect or ideal answer. Most of the situations entail alternatives that are both good and bad and we most often choose the best of the imperfect options. Having imperfect people and free choices, we will never completely avoid these situations on the earth. Maybe that's why people refer to it as Heaven – because most peoples' ideas of Heaven would not involve the harm that we perpetrate on one another on the earth.

I once read a saying in a book of quotations that I appreciated. The saying stated that contentment on earth belongs only to those with brutal or divine minds. In other words, only those who are divine enough to live with and above the spiritual atrocities committed or those who accept the spiritual atrocities because they are the ones performing them, are truly happy.

In any case, I fully believe that in the next world we will be able to forgive more easily, to grow ourselves, and to be free from the injustices and cruelties perpetrated on the earth. I would call such an environment Heaven.

Help from spirit

I recently was giving a reading to two mediums who are dear friends of mine going through trauma in their personal lives. I am passing on what their loved ones in spirit said, because their words of encouragement were also an inspiration to me, as they may be to others. Sometimes messages are universal.

I began by seeing three relatives in silhouette standing side-by-side and holding hands in a semi circle, and I heard the word "fortress". I got the message that they were lending support, providing a wall of defense, and my colleague, Harvey, saw them add a fourth person, not in spirit, and form a full circle, holding hands, indicating that they were standing together with their loved one who is in the physical and giving her encouragement.

I heard the words of John Lennon, that everything will be all right in the end, and if it's not all right, it's not the end. I then got the message that spirit can't always fix all of our problems, but sometimes the lesson in some of our most difficult physical trials is that we can't always resolve those problems in the way we would like, but they are spiritual challenges that provide us with soul growth in the sense that we must gain the strength to endure despite those problems.

Harvey added that spirit is there not to provide a solution or a definitive answer, and can't always change the outcome, but is there to inspire us and fortify us with their collective strength.

I was given two images, one of a woman with terminal cancer whom we had prayed for many years ago in a church I had attended, who subsequently went into remission and lived far beyond her life expectancy. This was a message regarding the power of collective intention and prayer. The second image was of a church I was affiliated with in my youth that had "prayer warriors", women who gathered at church in the daytime to pray collectively for those undergoing problems. This was a message about the strength of community effort, the concentrated thoughts and prayers of many.

Harvey then received the song, "You'll Never Walk Alone", indicating that when we are walking through dark places, we are so focused on the issue at hand, that it is hard to remember that we're not alone. It is always easy to feel connected to spirit when we are receiving a reading in circle, but we should also be aware that when we are preoccupied with troubles, they haven't deserted us. We are never alone.

The passage from the Bible about Joshua walking around the walls of Jericho seven times was given to me and Harvey sang the song, "Joshua Fought the Battle of Jericho, and the Walls Came Tumbling Down". To me, this image symbolized the spiritual strength and determination we need when the physical odds seem impossible. At this point I felt the vibration of love. It is difficult to describe, but I felt that emotion transmitted to me in my physical body. No words were given, as words are sometimes inadequate, and answers are not easy, but love, support, and encouragement were being given.

Harvey was given images of the Berlin Wall and the Great Wall of China, and said that physical walls don't mean as much as the power of people and physical walls eventually crumble.

Someone asked the question, "Why must we live through tragedy"? I received an impression of the accomplished Australian medium, Deb Webber, who once asked her guides why she had to undergo such a devastating first marriage, and said she was told that if we don't understand hatred we will never understand love. I took from this that we will never appreciate goodness, peace, love, or fully understand it, unless we experience the lack of these blessings, the opposite.

Before the reading ended, a spirit came through for the other medium. Her relative showed me the image of my friend walking on a tightrope, struggling and trying to balance without falling. Harvey saw her on a teeter totter. This exemplified the state of my friend's life at present. Then her loved one in spirit handed her a balancing pole, indicating the love and support spirit was sending her, and the spirit showed me my friend putting one foot in front of the other cautiously and systematically. The message was that my friend was trying to balance many different situations in her life simultaneously, that spirit was busy backing her up and supporting her, and that she couldn't just run off the tight rope and solve all her problems overnight, but needed to concentrate on one step at a time, difficult as it might seem. There was no miraculous solution, but, as in the parable of the turtle and the hare, slow and steady wins the race.

Although all of these comments came from my friends' loved ones in Spirit, I thought of how relevant these messages were, and of how I could apply them to my own life difficulties. Hopefully they may be an inspiration to you as they have been to me.

The Soul Knows

When I was young, I remember my mother telling me about an old radio program called, "The Shadow Knows". If I recall correctly, the line was, "What evil lurks in the hearts of men? The Shadow knows." Not to indicate any correlation with that old radio program, I feel the soul knows things that our conscious mind doesn't. Some people call it your sub-conscious mind, others your higher self, but I like to think of it as the soul.

I have had several incidents in which I believe I knew something inside of which I wasn't consciously aware. One was before my mother died. As she lay in her hospital bed, I felt a strong urge to tell her something personal about my life that she wasn't aware of. It was something I hadn't discussed with her over a period of 25 years, but I suddenly felt the need to talk about it. It was not long after that that my mother suffered an incident that was an acute turning point in her recovery and she went into a coma, dying three weeks later.

The second incident occurred before the death of my dog, Angel. I sometimes talk to my dogs even though I don't know how much they comprehend. My friend was an EMT for a long time and always talked to the patients whether or not they were conscious. He, himself, had been in a coma from meningitis when he was young, and could hear every word the doctors said, even though he couldn't respond and they thought he was oblivious.

Dogs can learn commands and language to an extent, and I believe they can sense emotions. So one day I felt impelled to sit down and say to my dog, "You know, we're both getting older. I love you. When we go, will you join me on the other side? Let's meet on the Rainbow Bridge." I don't know how much of it she understood but she jumped up and kissed me, and I was satisfied that that was a "yes." She was not critically ill and I never expected that she would die suddenly, unexpectedly and traumatically, less than a week later. Consciously, I had no premonition, but on a soul level, I felt impelled to have that last conversation with her. I had also taken a bunch of pictures of her several days before she died, and sent one to my friend, Harvey, which I had never done before.

I think, at times, our souls know things that we, as rational conscious human beings, don't.

HOW IT ALL STARTED

I was one of those kids who always wanted answers. Why are we here? What happens when we die? I'm named after my grandmother, Prudence, who was a medium. I call her a reluctant medium because she spontaneously developed the gift at the age of 16 without consciously seeking it. In those days, mediums were frequently ostracized, and, oftentimes, the kindest word used to describe them was "crazy". So my grandmother never used her gift professionally or sought to develop it. In fact, she was initially frightened when spirits visited her. At times she would become temporarily paralyzed or immobilized, going into what is described as a catatonic state just before she went to sleep. That is when spirits came to visit her. Most often they were people she didn't know, some benevolent, some mischievous, and sometimes people close to her like my deceased grandfather. She recognized some locations as being more paranormally active or conducive to communication. As I grew older and read about these phenomena, I realized that she was a physical medium, as occasionally spirits used her energy to move objects. She usually saw spirits from the waist up and occasionally could hear them speak.

I remember listening to her, fascinated, as she told me about a spirit who said to her, "Charlie Jones, Charlie Jones, it's so hard to come back." She was initially puzzled until she remembered her closest childhood friend, Charlotte Jones. I learned from that just how difficult it is for spirits to manifest themselves in the physical world, and my grandmother heard her clairaudiently, not as a disembodied physical voice.

My mother told me about the time when she was young that my grandmother was awakened from sleep by being "thrown" against a wall, later suffering bruises. Upon awakening she discovered a gas leak in the house, saving the entire family from death. Without those spirits who had helped my grandmother, I wouldn't be here to tell the story.

Years later my grandmother, doing automatic writing, received several messages from close friends of mine who had passed, whom she didn't know. In the first communication she received my friend's former address, which was unusual, because it had a ½ in the number portion of the address, and a message warning me about an upcoming potential danger in my life that was averted when I heeded his advice. The validity of the message was corroborated when a friend, who knew nothing of the message, later told me about a violent individual who had the intention of harming me. That message also included the name and appearance of the hospital where my friend died. To demonstrate that my grandmother didn't pick this information up from me telepathically, I thought it was incorrect and drove by the hospital to check. I had remembered the color of the brick incorrectly. My grandmother's message had it right.

Another message that came through my grandmother in automatic writing was from a different friend who had passed. I was very upset about the passing and he communicated through my grandmother his name, the words, "no mourning", and "love". My grandmother hadn't known of him, and what was even more astounding, the message came through in his handwriting, which she had never seen, not hers.

I also had several visitations in dreams from my late father, giving me information on important issues in my life. This all seemed normal to me because I grew up around it. But I never thought of myself as psychic or mediumistic.

Later, when my grandmother passed, all the relatives were gathered in the house, and in the middle of the night, some of the lights in the house, which had been out, began turning on and off by themselves, eliciting screams from my cousin. On another occasion, my mother was worried about my aunt, her sister, who was in Mayo clinic for a lung surgery. While my mother was sleeping at my cousin's house, the lights turned on by themselves at night in the bedroom where she was sleeping. She took this as a sign from my grandmother that all would be well regarding the surgery, and it was.

Several days after my mother passed, my former husband, who is now also on the other side, experienced a lamp turning on which wasn't even plugged in. Having lived with me, he immediately felt this was my mother letting us know she was okay. So that is how, before all the tv shows and books on the subject, I learned that spirits can communicate through electricity and electronic devices.

Although I've had a lifelong fascination with the paranormal, and a burning desire to know what is on the other side of the veil of death, I didn't begin pursuing my own development until I had a devastating loss. Getting his name from John Edward's website, I made an appointment with British medium, Robert Brown. After the reading, I thought it was just a coincidence when he invited me to join him in a mediumship training course, where he had one spot left open. I was scared to death, standing on the platform in front of all those people, never having given anyone a message before. But Spirit helped me to say some things that made sense. At that time I didn't know that there are no coincidences or that all of us have latent abilities of clairvoyance, clairsentience, claircognizance, and clairaudience, which can be developed. We really are all spirits having a human experience.

Since that time a friend and I have been pursuing further training in a Spirit circle and in courses given by other well known mediums. I have been on several "ghost hunts" with A.J. Barrera, a Southern California medium with his own television and radio shows, on the Queen Mary and at historical churches. I had the opportunity to use the spirit box, Ovilus, and full spectrum camera. At one meeting, Nancy Myers, the "orb lady", took a picture of me and showed it to me on the spot. It contained an orb over my shoulder with an image of my dog Holly, who had recently passed.

One extraordinarily evidential communication came through my friend, Harvey. I was depressed that evening because the grapevine was closed and we couldn't get to E's spirit circle in L.A., so we decided to meditate. Afterward, when I asked my friend what he got, he said, "Oh, just something crazy, that doesn't make any sense." Well, they always tell mediums not to judge, just to give what they get. So I said to Harvey, what was it? He said, "I saw two women standing in a kitchen. One looked like a young Julia Child, and she threw her hands up in the air and said, 'Well, I guess we'll just have to bake an elephant cake.'" Of course that sounded crazy to Harvey, but my mouth fell open. That was a personal symbol between my deceased loved one and myself, something only the two of us knew. And, if that's not enough, a young medium in training whom I met for the first time in Alta Dena, California, and who knew nothing about me, gave me a reading and asked my why my mother was giving me an elephant trunk.

I have had so many incredible experiences that have given me peace and hope, as well as the desire to help others to have comfort in their grief. I respect both mediums and paranormal investigators, both working on two sides of the same coin to demonstrate the continuation of life.

I was using software to record EVP's with a background of a white noise loop. I was mentally talking to my deceased loved one and said, "As long as I know you're okay, and that our love continues, I won't worry about anything." When I listened to my recording, right after my comment, his voice was captured, saying, in a class A EVP, "That's the best."

After Robert Brown told me my loved one was working hard to manifest himself to me in the physical, I am now able at times to feel his "electromagnetic touch", a tingling electrical charge or mild shock that is definitely discernible, not from me, and confirming something he has said to me. I have also been able to feel him as a force moving my arm or hand, even more powerful where there is group energy in mediumship circles.

I've since read that we sign soul contracts in the afterlife regarding our lessons and what we plan to accomplish in this life. At any given time, we are right where we are meant to be. One medium I respect, Austyn Wells, said never to ask why did this happen to me, but instead of seeing ourselves as victims, to ask why did this happen for me? In other words, what lesson can I take from this, or what positive thing did I learn, even from a negative experience? A sitter on Long Island Medium got a message from his father, "Don't look at them as mistakes, but as lessons learned."

Purportedly communicating through the late medium Geraldine Cummins, psychic researcher, F.W.H. Myers said, "We are placed in the physical to develop the spiritual." I believe that we are all on this journey, contributing in our own unique ways, to this great unending adventure.

THE SOUL

How would you describe the soul?

Communicated through Harvey 8/17/16

The soul is the essence of the Spirit. Away from the trappings of life, it is the pure spirit tied to a supreme being.

The soul is eternal, as is the spirit. They are parallel entities. The soul is a gift from God.

Recognizing and Dealing with Negative Influences

After I opened up spiritually, I began to have sporadic negative dreams. They were nightmares that left me sobbing. Their content was usually reliving the worst thing that has ever happened to me in my life, or seeing it recur in the future. They left me shaken and deeply affected, and it often took a greater part of the day to reestablish normalcy.

They had never occurred before I opened up spiritually, and I was puzzled. Was I just reliving and trying to mentally cope with the past, as a psychologist friend suggested? Were my guides giving them to me to encourage me to address some lesson I needed to learn, or to gain strength?

I got a clue one night when I had a lucid dream, like the visitations you get from loved ones in spirit – very vivid, where you can actually hear them talking. But this time it didn't come from loved ones. I clearly heard in my dream the words, "Why don't you just kill yourself?" I knew it didn't come from me or from my loved ones or guides.

Since that time I have had occasional instances during which I hear a negative comment in my mind that I know without question didn't come from me. I can see why some people experiencing the paranormal say that they fear they are going crazy. If you are sensitive you are open to spirits — good or bad — and must protect yourself against the bad ones.

I knew without a doubt that these negative comments were coming from negative spirits or entities. That is when I contacted my guides to ask for advice on how to protect myself from negative influence. I reasoned, if this is happening to me, I'm sure it's happening to others also.

The advice that Harvey and I got from our guides is recorded on the following pages.

When those who are sensitive and open to spirit occasionally hear very negative comments in their minds that they know didn't come from them, who do these comments come from – demons or negative spirits? And how do you stop them?

Communicated to Harvey on 11/12/16

When we do not close down after a spirit session, it is similar to leaving the front door of your house unlocked and ajar after leaving.

You do not have to be in the home of a negative spirit or demon to be affected by their energy. The more exposure you have to negatives, the better the chance of being drawn into their energy.

In a spirit reading, we ask for protection, and the white light of God, and the guides we have also add a filtering effect for negative energy. As we get further away from a spirit contact, the filter effect fades, and we become more open to negatives that we did not invite.

In that case, we must confront the energy and uninvite them from our space and our consciousness. And we must forbid them from future contacts.

We have the ability to replace evil with good. These contacts come from dark places, and we have the ability to send them back to their source.

Harvey made several comments upon the information he channeled. He concluded that when you forget to close down properly or protect yourself adequately, this is an unwritten invitation for negative entities to come in and wreak havoc, just as much as failing to lock the doors of your house permits criminals to intrude and rob you.

He indicated that some suicides may be influenced by such negative entities as well. Those who are unsuspecting or unaware may be tormented, and those whose defenses are down may be controlled by negative spirits. Some negative entities are even solicited or welcomed in.

Negative Communication

When someone who is open to spirit occasionally hears negative comments in their mind that they know do not come from them – who do these comments come from – demons or negative spirits? And how do you stop them?

Communicated through Penny on 11/12/16

Negative comments can come from someone outside of you, either negative spirits or other non-human negative entities, and they often come at a time when you are most vulnerable.

We are not infallible, but attempt to make a blanket of protection around those we guide. I do not know the origin of all those thoughts. Others beyond me or above me may find out.

First, do not be influenced by them. Say that they are not from you and do not be influenced by them. Build up your own inner resources and try to be more positive. Know where these comments are coming from – from unloving spirits, from negative spirits, not from those who love you. Reach out to those who love you, guide you, and protect you. Ask those who are in the spirit world at the vibration of love to guide and protect you – even God. All of those help, praying for help from angels and religious figures.

If negative spirits are attempting to damage a relationship of love with someone you care for, talk about it, discuss it, and both of you must agree to not let it influence you, and then you can reject and dismiss it. Set your own boundaries with your intentions and prayer, and this also involves asking for those who love and guide you in spirit to protect you with boundaries.

Yes, someone negative can occasionally penetrate those boundaries, but not as easily. If a negative thought does occur that you feel is not from you, both of you must agree to let it go and not acknowledge it.

It is a work in progress. That's why the Bible says "watch and pray". Remember the parable in the Bible about Jesus with the devil coming to him with challenges three times. If the devil doesn't give up, we must not give up. Jesus said, "The servant is not greater than his lord. If they have persecuted me, they will also persecute you."

That is why the Bible admonishes us to put on the full armor of God to resist the fiery darts of the wicked. It also states, "Watch, fight, and pray," and, "Fight the good fight of faith." Martin Luther writes, "One with God is a majority." Pray always. Recall the sovereignty of the soul. You are in a collaboration with God. Do not give place to the devil.

When you're tired, depressed, overworked, or in conflict internally or with other people, you are more vulnerable. You must close down properly when you open up the readings. If something or someone negative comes through, vociferously repudiate it. Be firm and stand in spiritual strength. The Bible states, "Resist the devil, and the devil will flee from you."

PAST LIFE RELATIONSHIPS

Will we meet in the afterlife?

Communicated through Penny on 8/17/16

If people wish to meet, they will. We meet those who were active participants in our lives, those with whom we are engaged in learning.

Only those we truly love do we remain with, but we meet those who played significant roles in our lives to discuss what we learned from one another – those we influenced and those who influenced us. We meet those who came to earth to teach us.

We are required to review our choices and their consequences. We will meet those who helped us and those who challenged us. We are always connected, but do not necessarily remain together.

Those who shared our path for a while are required to meet only if we played a significant role in one another's lives.

If we choose to find someone, we can. We are always trying to advance and those who helped us to advance by playing either a negative or positive role, we acknowledge and thank.

No one is alone. We all interact together as we also do on the other side. Our thoughts and goals draw those to us who are of like mind.

Absolute Truth

Is there such a thing as absolute truth, absolute values of right and wrong?

Communicated through Harvey 8/19/16

For humankind, there are no absolutes. They are fallible and free will allows for fallibility.

As humans, we strive for Nirvana, but it is just beyond our fingertips.

Different cultures allow for a myriad of acceptable behaviors as pure, but they are not universally acceptable.

After we cross, we go through a series of cleansing levels, to establish a baseline of acceptable behavior and levels. As we draw closer to Source, we understand the ability to draw closer to perfection.

There are no absolutes on earth.

PEOPLE FROM PRIOR LIFETIMES

Can we contact people from previous lifetimes?

Communicated through Penny 8/19/16

We can know who we were involved with in our history. We can know them and talk to them. We are able to communicate with those from our prior lifetimes. We are always linked with them.

If they have advanced to a higher plane, we can contact them with our thought and they can come to us or communicate with us. We do not necessarily go to them in that case.

If they are in a physical incarnation, we can communicate with their soul, but not necessarily with their conscious mind, so to speak.

As long as we are able to communicate with them mentally, geographic distance is not a hindrance. We are all linked, even to God. There are no typical barriers of distance or time.

We do know those we have interacted with. We will recognize them in our soul form. No two souls are barred from each other if they wish to interact. We are advised and recommended courses of action beneficial for us, but not inhibited from free will of association.

We all have our own soul associations and different relationships with them. We also can make new acquaintances.

We can all access our prior lives, thoughts, and actions, and can discuss our past lives together if we wish. No one is left without a record of their life. We have our own soul memories we can recall, and can also access records of our lives in the Akashic records.

SPIRITUAL LESSONS

What are the spiritual lessons we are supposed to learn in the afterlife?

Communicated through Harvey 8/21/16

We must learn patience and tolerance. We must learn to love ourselves, and give freely to all entities.

We must learn to forgive our negative behaviors that we left behind, before we can accept healing and advance to a purer realm than that which we arrived upon.

When we arrive on earth again, we might be tempted with the same temptations, but we will be able to make better choices.

RELIVING LESSONS

Why after advancing through several levels in the afterlife and after multiple reincarnations, must we relive some of the trials and tribulations of our prior life?

Communicated through Penny 8/21/16

If we learned everything in one lifetime, we wouldn't have to come back. We are always perfecting ourselves. No single lesson we learn guarantees perfection. We need to prove ourselves within the physical world. No lesson is complete until it is tested.

We will not be re-challenged with some of our major lessons after we have proven our understanding. Some lessons we are faced with we learn completely, some partially, and some not at all. We, ourselves, choose our lessons with divine input.

We may be challenged with a similar lesson we have mastered in order to help others see or witness through us how to handle a similar problem themselves.

Some lessons are inherent in the nature of physical life, such as illness, loss through death, job and family issues, and we will have some repetitive issues because of the structure and framework of physical life.

Also, we may wish to address a different aspect of the same lesson, or have to help others address that problem.

When we have completely mastered a particular lesson, we will not have to repeat it unless we choose to in order to teach others. Maybe the larger issue is love, but we have to address many of its facets, such as forgiveness, patience, compromise, etc. The lesson may fall under the greater category but be a different permutation within that category.

We may also undergo a similar lesson so we can be an example to others or teach others to grow.

SPIRITS AND EUPHORIA

The feelings of euphoria and bliss given to D, K, and I by spirits - do spirits on the other side have those feelings occasionally or all the time?

Communicated through Harvey 8/27/16

Euphoria is a human emotion caused by a release of endorphins in the brain. These feelings can be fleeting and caused by a revelation, a human event, or a pleasurable spirit contact.

In the afterlife, mood swings are redundant. We can experience pleasurable times and contacts at will.

SPIRIT SIGHTINGS

When people on earth see spirits or past events, are they seeing this with their normal senses or are they seeing this clairvoyantly?

Communicated through Harvey 8/28/16

Spirits and trace images from past events can be seen by many people. Some events have been witnessed and related word by word by mediums and nonbelievers.

Events and spirits can be viewed by sight or clairvoyantly depending upon the strength of the spirits.

MEMORIES OF PRIOR LIVES

When we return to the afterlife, do we retain memories of any previous incarnations?

Communicated through Penny 8/29/16

We are aware of our whole record. We are aware of other lives but don't recall all the details. We all have some knowledge of prior lifetimes and former associations. Also, we are aware of our most important lessons. We have knowledge of the lives we have lived, but do not necessarily recall all the details.

We are able to realize all of these things if we wish, as they are a permanent record in our soul. If we wish to review or relive a specific past event or memory, we are able to access that record and review or relive it.

All of the details of our long history are not foremost in our consciousness, but we are aware of the major events of prior lives and prior soul associations. Although not all of our memories are in our conscious awareness at all times, we can retrieve personal memories or gain access to them through the Akashic records. Both methods are available.

It is like the recall we have when suddenly remembering a name or detail of a past event that we wish to remember. We have a record of all these past memories in our souls, and can recall them if we wish or gain access to or retrieve our previous lifetimes through the eternal record of the Akashia. We can obtain information as we wish and need.

We are also aware of past soul connections. We have records that are available to us at all times and even our own personal recall is good. Those memories are a part of us. We can actually see and feel those past events again as we lived them.

ARE SPIRITS EVER ANNIHILATED?

Are any spirits ever reprocessed or do they lose their identity and start over as described in the lake of fire in the Bible?

Communicated through Harvey 8/30/16

As we ascend to the afterlife, it becomes plain that no spirits are all good or all bad. As humans we all bend to temptations. Some of us are able to atone for our transgressions during our time on earth, and some cannot.

It is possible to make amends after our time in the afterlife. Spirits can be purified as we ascend through the levels above.

DO WE REMEMBER EARTH LIVES?

Do we recall our earth life when we enter the afterlife?

Communicated through Penny 8/30/16

At the time of transition from earth, we are still aware of our life on earth as we enter the afterlife. We are aware of what happened to us. We even know more about it than we did when we were on earth.

We are aware of how other people acted, they are aware of how we acted, and both are aware of how the other felt.

We remember our lives very clearly. We recall how we felt and what we did. We are even able to recall details if we wish or learn circumstances of prior lives. We can mentally relive situations if we want to.

We can recall much of our past lives or even look into the Akashic records at prior events that made us who we are. If we want to, we can talk with others who were with us, or spiritual advisers, about what we did or didn't do and how we could have better handled situations.

We see threads of cause and effect in our lives and the effects of karma. We also know where we need to work on ourselves.

MEDIUMSHIP READINGS OF THE LIVING

When a medium communicates with a spirit and that person turns out to be alive, but they not only get information about them which could be obtained psychically from the sitter, but get a message from that living person, how does that happen?

Communicated through Harvey 9/2/16

While it is possible that part of the reading may be a psychic reading, it is also possible that a message may come from an older generation (Father's father). We often cannot initially identify which generation is coming through in a reading, and we often get more than one spirit in a reading.

A spirit may take the opportunity to come on the energy of an earthly spirit.

It is also possible that part of the psychic reading reflected the remorse of the earthly spirit for his transgressions.

OBE'S AND FOREKNOWLEDGE OF DEATH

For those of us who have had OBE's, and have stood in the light, will we know when the silver cord will be severed?

Communicated through Penny on 9/2/16

It all depends on the situation. Some of us who have had traumatic deaths don't even realize we're dead. That can also apply to some spirits who were mentally impaired at the time of their death.

When a death is anticipated, those who are helpers and loved ones in the afterlife prepare for it and facilitate the separation of the spirit body from the physical, and assist the transition over. In those cases, the crossing spirit will be aware that they are transitioning but may not feel very different initially.

It also depends upon the level of spiritual awareness of the dying person, with an easier and more comprehensible transition for those who are spiritually evolved. They become aware they are not in the body and not seen or heard by those in the physical world.

They can be instantly or gradually aware that they have made the transition. It's all in the awareness of the individual.

If they are greatly debilitated and near death for a long time or die instantaneously and traumatically, they may not even be aware the cord has been severed.

In well facilitated deaths, the dying person may be aware of spiritual helpers assisting them in leaving the body and breaking the cord.

Some may remain near the earth for a while, depending on the strength of their desire. Others may see deceased loved ones waiting for them and others may abruptly or swiftly pass through the tunnel to the other side.

It's easy to tell when your cord is broken because you can't return into the body. When you see your dead body and can't get back in, you realize you're dead.

If we have an OBE and are offered a choice of transitioning to the afterlife or returning to earth, we will know that choosing to stay in the afterlife necessitates breaking of the cord.

For those who return to their earth life, like all others, some may have premonitions that the time of their death is near while others may not be aware. On a soul level it is not uncommon to have intuitions of our imminent departure. In either case, for those who have experienced OBE's, their concept of death is forever altered.

CLARITY OF MEDIUMSHIP COMMUNICATION

What methods can you use to enhance the clarity of the communication from the other side and to differentiate the spirit's message from your own thoughts?

Communicated through Harvey 9/3/16

First, proper grounding and meditation to arrive at a quiet place, to clear your head of the normal mundane clutter.

Allow the message to arrive without trying to make sense or edit it. Try for a clear connection with spirit by arriving in a quiet place and only hearing from spirit, remaining passive, and not generating thoughts in your own mind.

ADVICE/WARNINGS FROM GUIDES

Some mediums, like the famous psychic detective in New Zealand, Kelvin Cruickshank, have guides who warn them of danger or even alert them to beware of certain romantic relationships. Why don't we all get advice like that from our guides? Why only some people?

Communicated through Harvey 9/6/16

I feel that some mediums mistake their gut feelings, psychically, for a warning from their guides. Since my guides only speak to me during a reading, I have never experienced warnings directly during or before an upcoming event. Our guides are here to guide, not direct.

MEETING OUR GUIDES IN THE AFTERLIFE

Will we meet our guides face to face in the afterlife?

Communicated through Penny 9/6/16

We will have very close communication with our guides. We will be able to discuss our life with him/her/them. They will be able to discuss what we've done, what challenges we faced, and how we addressed them.

You will have a very intense "de-programming" with your guide. You will be helped to overcome the traumas and emotional baggage of earth life.

If you wish to, you will be able to see them in a human form. You will know your previous relations and associations with them from the afterlife and/or any prior lives.

If you both agree to it, you can both continue to have a communication or relationship.

Your guide will be right with you, as well as other spiritual teachers, when you have your life review, supporting and helping with service.

Guides are souls who have mastered certain situations in their lives and are able to help others address similar problems. Each has a different awareness and knowledge, and many act in concert to assist in an individual's development.

They can be very close, such as a relative or a loved one, or they may be a stranger who has a special interest to impart. Your main guide is dedicated to you personally, and has a deep connection with you. Sometimes your guide will remain affiliated with you and your growth in the afterlife, or progress to do other work.

SPIRITUAL VALUES

What are the spiritual values we must learn for progression?

Communicated through Penny on 9/10/16

For those who wish to move up the levels, purify themselves, and progress on the other side, what are the spiritual lessons or principles/values they must learn?

How do you want to be treated? Positive values include humility, strength, fortitude, courage, kindness, gentleness, helpfulness, charity, compassion, caring, unselfishness, patience, long-suffering, forgiveness, mercy, tolerance, faithfulness, commitment, dedication, honesty, self-respect and respect for others, fairness, justice, faith, hope, and love.

Do no intentional harm; avoid malice, theft, lies, cheating, exploitation, violence, and substance addiction. Help others to learn and progress. Seek to overcome obstacles. Nurture spiritual rather than materialistic values. Practice the "Golden Rule."

When we have problems or difficulties, we should persevere through them and try to make things work out the best for all involved.

PRECOGNITION

Do we know in our soul future events such as the time of our death? Why do some people seem to know this?

Communicated through Harvey 9/13/16

Some souls when they arrive on earth are destined to have a short time on this plane. Some have an inner premonition of their lack of longevity. They are prompted to complete their mission on earth in the time allotted.

REINCARNATION

When in the afterlife, at which level, can we be reincarnated?

Communicated through Penny on 9/13/16

At all levels until we rejoin Source we can reincarnate. We are more likely to be reincarnated when we are at the lower levels in order to gain experience more quickly and to progress.

At level five we cease to need to reincarnate. We have a different mission when we reincarnate depending upon the level we are at. When we are at level four, we typically reincarnate for humanitarian service more than for our own personal development. That, in a form, does represent development for us. It is a mission of service.

People at the upper levels can also reincarnate by choice to fulfill a certain need to help humanity, but their choice is optional. Those at lower levels do not have to reincarnate but usually do so to learn lessons that cannot be readily or quickly attained on the other side.

It should also be remembered that even in the afterlife, as having form and a certain kind of substance, although different from the human body, as we progress through the levels we really are successively incarnating until we reunite with Source, at which time we no longer have a separate, independent form.

FORGIVENESS AND MOVING ON

In a recent television show, Morgan Fairchild was given apologies from the other side from souls who couldn't move forward until she forgave them. Another medium channeled a spirit who said you have to "make things right" on the other side. If we planned our lives and lessons on the other side to learn from them – from the consequences, why do we need to forgive one another if these problems were planned by us to learn from them in the first place?

Communicated through Harvey 9/16/16

Because we have the ability to exercise free will, every second of our time on earth is not pre-scripted.

Also, our contact with other souls may not mesh seamlessly with the plans made for our lessons on earth. When we deviate from our plan on earth, we may have to apologize for our transgressions, and forgive any transgressions we may have experienced.

SPIRIT APPEARANCE

How do we recognize the souls we knew on earth on the other side? Do they present themselves in a way they looked when we knew them? How do we know them if they look younger or like they did in another incarnation, or even like a ball of light?

Communicated through Penny 9/16/16

When we communicate thoughts, we communicate our old identity. We have the ability to talk to each other. We know each other not because we look the same or have a voice or set appearance, but by our personality and memories.

We can project the prior image of ourselves or a prior voice, and communicate by thoughts who we were. We can make ourselves known if we wish to. We can project ourselves as we used to be if we want.

We have our own unique consciousness – identity – our energy is a signature, an identifier. We are able to "read "and "transmit" one another's energy that is recognized as a unique vibrational signature like a name would be on earth.

By thinking of the person you knew, you automatically connect with their spirit, regardless of what they look or sound like.

No one can deceive someone on the other side or impersonate someone else. They can look like that person or present themselves like someone else, but we know their thoughts – so deceit is not a factor. Thoughts and feelings are transparent – not hidden behind a mask as on earth. We recognize each other by our own unique conscious energy and thoughts – the real you. It's like meeting an old friend on earth. You share memories, know their personality, quirks, traits, and that lasting part you will recognize.

MORAL VALUES

Do all souls on the other side agree about morality, such as capital punishment, lying, stealing, divorce, adultery, etc., or do they disagree as we do on earth?

Communicated through Harvey 9/20/16

Upon arrival in the spirit world, wrongdoing is not an option. Immorality is left on the earth plane and is not something that is open for debate.

Our soul is there to be purified. Therefore, our prejudices and negative thoughts are left behind.

NDE'S AND PREDESTINATION

During a near death experience, do we really have a choice to come back, or is it a pre-destined experience to teach us faith?

Communicated through Penny 7/20/16

Most of those who have a near death experience have it for a purpose. They have a mission to accomplish. It is meant to change their lives and direct them on a more spiritual path of enlightenment, and to affect the lives of those they contact. In those cases they are told they must return.

Others are given the choice to progress on the other side or to return to their physical life to fulfill their purpose or to complete their life plans and experience – the chance to fulfill their earthly goals.

Sometimes near death experiences are the result of accident, tragedy, or chance, and sometimes they are written into our soul purpose to prompt us to progress or fulfill our destiny in a different way.

If they are accidental, we often have a choice to depart or return, but if they are predestined we often are required to return to fulfill our life's purpose.

They can be accidental or predestined. In either case, we may be required to return to earth to fulfill our life's purpose. If predestined, they often serve to give us spiritual enlightenment and are a catalyst to direct us and those whose lives we touch on a more spiritual path.

If accidental, and we have fulfilled the greater part of our life's purpose, we may be given the chance to progress on the other side or to continue on earth to fulfill our life experiences and goals.

Non-Human Spirits

Are there spirits that have never been incarnated in any physical incarnation?

Communicated through Penny 9/21/16

All souls are created by God with a purpose, a divine intention. They are each given a separate existence with an individual consciousness for a specific purpose.

There are some that have not chosen to incarnate on the earth plane or other levels of similar density. Some have been given tasks of assisting God without a mortal incarnation. All creatures not experiencing a human incarnation might be considered angels, but are not angels in the conventional human interpretation.

There are echelons of souls, and many are not involved in human incarnations. Many are assistants of God in other realms and oversee the evolution of advancing souls.

We all have a purpose. Not all of us have the same purpose. Those of the advanced realms who have never had a physical incarnation have not been exposed to the negativity of the earth plane, nor does it apply to them. Although those souls have free will, they are not in a situation where they can express negativity unless they undergo a physical incarnation or attempt to influence those in a physical incarnation.

Evil comes from a soul's intentions and consciousness, and is an aspect of free will, but for that soul to influence others, that soul must be incarnated in a dimension that permits the perpetration of evil or they may be in a lower spiritual plane that they utilize to influence others with negativity. It does exist but not in the realms of higher vibration.

All souls are created pure, but some are exposed to the free will environments, and, as such, must learn by choice and progress.

There are other environments within the infinite creation that are subject to negativity as the earth. If spirits have negative thoughts, intentions, and vibrations, they are not permitted to dwell at the higher frequency levels. Their vibration of thought and consciousness selects their level. If they choose to, they are able to exercise their free will to change. All creation is dynamic and no soul is denied progress.

CONSENSUS ON RIGHT AND WRONG

Do all souls agree on what is wrong and what is right – like the 10 Commandments?

Communicated through Harvey 9/25/16

No. We bring our baggage to the afterlife and must sort out our paths (right or wrong) from our life on earth, with guidance from our guides and teaching spirits.

LIFE REVIEW

When we die and look over our lives, how do we know what we did wrong and what we did right?

Communicated through Harvey 9/25/16

In the afterlife, right and wrong are subjective, governed by cause and effect. Sometimes an action may harm another, and sometimes the same action may help another.

If we follow our heart and strive to do the right thing, it is considered to be right, even if the result is not positive. We are given support from our guides to determine right and wrong.

DIVIDED SOULS

Can a spirit on the other side divide itself and become two people on earth and then reunite as one soul in the afterlife?

Communicated through Penny 9/25/16

They can create another soul that is part of them but yet unique, formed from their own mental energy, but operating independently for a specified interval. They can experience separate existences in separate physical bodies, and then reunite as they return to the other side.

As we are able to reunite and merge consciousness with God, so we are able to reunite with another soul. We are able to reunite our consciousness in a merger that allows us to combine the expression and memories of both physical incarnations. It's like having different experiences in different times of your life, but they are all a part of you.

One can recombine a consciousness that was originally one. Souls can divide for the purpose of advancing their progression more rapidly, to ensure their continued progress as with twin flames, and then remerge into one identity.

All those who choose to do so are able to do so. God created twin flames to help each other in their development. God had intentions of reuniting them after their physical incarnations are complete. But we all have free will. We are able to retain separate consciousness if we wish.

On the other side, souls can temporarily divide their consciousness in order to be in two "places" at once. Geographic distance and time do not have the same limitations, restrictions, and barriers that they have in the physical world.

PURPOSE

What is our purpose? Are we all different or the same?

Communicated through Penny 9/25/17

People have different purposes and some have different missions. God creates us with a purpose in mind. Although we all have the same types of lessons to learn, each has unique capabilities and talents.

We each employee our God-given talents in a purpose for the forwarding and advancement, the betterment of the whole. No one is an island.

We empower the self to improve the whole, and to be in a position to help improve others. It's all part of God's plan. Within that plan we maintain individual freedoms.

ANIMAL SPIRITS

Can animal spirits ever incarnate as humans or do species always remain the same?

Communicated through Harvey 9/27/16

As it is possible for human spirits to be reincarnated as male or female, white or many colors and religions, it is possible under some circumstances for animals that had close interaction with humans on earth to be reincarnated as other species, i.e., animal or human. It is not a common occurrence, but is possible.

AKASHIC RECORDS

How do we access the Akashic records to obtain information from our past lives that may help us overcome problems or deal with troubled relationships in our current life?

Communicated through Harvey 9/30/16

The information in the records is within our subconscious mind at the time of our incarnation. The experiences in this earth plane are within our present memory, and will be passed on in the afterlife.

Accessing the records will not help in this realm, and we can exercise free will to alter our path on earth.

HAPPY INCARNATIONS

Can we ever have a happy or peaceful incarnation, not just a tumultuous or tormented one?

Communicated through Penny 7/30/16

If we have had a lot of difficult incarnations, we can have a happy one in which we use our abilities to have a positive effect upon others and not have a great degree of suffering.

If we are advanced, we can have a happy incarnation, as we have overcome many of our frailties and personality flaws, or weaknesses, and direct our efforts to helping others by instruction or example.

We all need a rest at times. That would be considered an incarnation of rest. If we wish to have such an incarnation, it would be made available for us.

That incarnation is directed more at helping others with their issues than in dealing with our own. We often seek incarnations that are difficult for our own more rapid development.

RELEVANCY OF RIGHT AND WRONG

Do spirits all agree on what is right and wrong when they get to the afterlife? Are right and wrong no longer relevant since spirits are not in a position to do wrong?

Communicated through Penny 9/30/16

None of us know all of the truth instantly when we come across. It is a process of learning on the other side as it is on earth. If we were instantly perfected, there would be no need to reincarnate. And if everything we expressed on earth and the moral issues were irrelevant when we come across, there would be no need for a life review for the purpose of remembering our experiences and lessons, and no need for some spirits to observe people on earth to see how they handle situations.

No, we can't do wrong in the afterlife, but that is not the point. If learning right and wrong were not important or irrelevant, what's the purpose of coming to earth to learn lessons in the first place or the point of having a life review to discuss those lessons?

We have a much clearer picture of right and wrong when we get to the afterlife. We know how what we did affected ourselves and others. We see the outcome of our choices.

Some spirits discuss working things out in the afterlife. If our previous actions were irrelevant why would there be a need to forgive or work things out? We don't have a clear-cut answer for every question, even in the afterlife. There is still room for a difference of opinion. We see alternatives and learn other choices, but no situation is all black or white and each choice has different consequences.

There is often no clear-cut black or white answer or choice once someone has done wrong. We are working in the spectrum of choices, trying to recognize the best alternative in our earthly environment where none are perfect because we are all involved in a network of choices affected by and affecting others, and cannot control all the circumstances or parameters. No one on earth is capable of living a life of perfection, as there are so many variables.

We perfect ourselves slowly and discuss issues, but our issues become less of a wall and more of a road bump. We learn of our flaws and seek to act more from love and for the welfare of all, including others and ourselves.

SPIRIT COMMUNICATION

What are spirit bodies and how do spirits communicate without a physical body?

Communicated through Penny 10/2/16

As we are energy, we determine our own form. We don't have a fixed form like we did on earth. We have a body, but it's not like the body we have on earth. It's a spirit body, one we can manipulate. We have a substance of sorts, but not an earthly substance.

We can look like a person if we want to. It's all determined by our own choices. We don't have to be in the body, but we still maintain form. It's not just a mental projection or thought. It's more than that.

We can project ourselves as we wish but we do have a form of substance. It's not just a thought projection or mirage. It's a real substance, just vibrating at a different rate or frequency, not visible within the spectrum of the human eye.

Yes, we can see each other. It's not just something we imagine. We are able to feel, see, and hear each other, but don't need the sensory apparatus of the human body to do so. We control our environment and ourselves more directly through our thoughts. We have more creative freedom, more control.

We create and manipulate our own reality with much more freedom, without the boundaries, limits, and restrictions of human experience. We have more power. We experience things as we wish them to be. We have more freedom of choice and a responsive environment – that's our prerogative.

We become more sensitive to our environment when we are out of the body. We don't need the sound waves of speech to capture thought, nor the pressure receptors of touch to experience sensation, nor the electromagnetically activated cells of the retina to form an image to experience sight. We directly process the sensory input of touch, hearing, sight, sound, and smell by our mind's apprehension of their properties, by the electromagnetic energy induction. The mental, visual, auditory, and tactile expression is an electromagnetic event.

Just like earth sight is an electrically transmitted visual expression, our mind is a receiving station for the visual impression or awareness that receives the electromagnetic impression of a visualized image, a perceived auditory sound or event, the sensed tactile stimulation. It is the electromagnetic impression or event that is created, perceived directly, and interpreted as sensory data would be on earth, incoming information that we decode and perceive as an image, a sound or a feeling, including emotion and understanding. These are being transmitted and received directly, not as they are on earth.

My awareness is even higher, more acute, than it was before. Communication is more direct, more intimate.

We have a way of expressing ourselves to facilitate communication and apprehension, understanding, the process of mental awareness and analysis, interpretation and knowledge. The interpretation, processing, and analysis of data that comes in to form an opinion, to understand a truth, to form an abstract concept or conclusion, to interpret behavior and attitude, to draw a conclusion, create an intellectual or emotional construct, an awareness or insight, is facilitated by direct transference of thoughts, emotions and impressions in the spirit world.

With all that said and done, the intellectual explanations, what is important is how we experience things together, how we interact, and what we know and feel.

GUIDES

Guides — how do they help us and why do some people have more conscious awareness of their connections with their guides and others seem to be given more direct recommendations from their guides?

Communicated through Penny 10/2/16

Guides are here to help, to inspire, and to aid the person and help them stay on their path. We can impart wisdom and give help in enlightening people with solutions and information they have requested. We cannot give warnings or information that will prevent or circumvent something that is meant to happen.

We cannot give warnings that will prevent someone from making mistakes and learning their needed lessons.

We can't suppress free will.

We can help to keep a person on their designated path and help if a situation threatens them or may cause them to be derailed from their life's plan.

We can influence and help if someone appeals to us for advice in a difficult situation or if a person wants to change for the better.

Guides can help, warn, and play an active role but cannot interfere with a pre-ordained life path, prevent mistakes and life lessons from being learned, or override free will.

We can hint, support, inspire, encourage, and assist a person in learning and in staying on their planned path, in learning and improving or progressing. Our suggestions and inspiration are always available, but a person must request or seek that information and be willing to listen and change, to implement the advice into their actions.

SOUL GROUP

What is your soul group like, for example, how many members are there, how often does the group usually reincarnate, what level are they on in the afterlife?

Communicated through Harvey 10/2/16

I have no knowledge of my soul group, or how it was formed (determined). Therefore I cannot answer the questions about its size or level of reincarnation.

Channeled by Harvey's guides.

DÉJÀ VU

Is the experience of déjà vu a memory of a past life or a psychic reading or a current experience?

Communicated through Penny 10/2/16

If there is an unusually strong draw to a location or you have knowledge of a place not explained by your current life experience, it usually indicates a prior life connection.

Places that have a history of a traumatic event or strong emotional "place memory," can also trigger feelings or images in those who are sensitive or mediums.

If you feel an intense and unexplained emotional draw to a place or uncanny knowledge of it, you are usually experiencing a past life memory. It is an inner conviction that the memory is yours, that you are connected, an unexplained "recall", a gut feeling, a pull that resonates with you deeply, either in a positive or negative way.

Place memories may be vivid but have no individual sense of "drawing" magnetic connection, or a feeling of personal involvement. They are those of an observer more than the feeling of a participant.

CONFLICTING MESSAGES

Why do different guides and mediums give very different answers to the same question?

Communicated through Penny 10/2/16

We have different opinions on the other side, too, as well as different levels of development and understanding. That is what makes us individual souls. Our individuality is reflected in the answers we give, and there may also be an influence from the prejudices, personality, and mindset of the channeling medium.

FEELINGS OF EUPHORIA

Feelings of Euphoria

The feelings of euphoria given to me and to D by different spirits were definitely not a product of a bodily chemical reaction triggered by an event. My experience occurred spontaneously and in a random situation with no preceding event, contact, or trigger, and originated from outside of me. It was a feeling of complete rapture that did not originate within me, that was given to me by someone outside of myself. My loved one on the other side spoke to me after the onset of these feelings, and I knew that they originated from him, not from me. The explanation of an endorphin high precipitated by some event in my life does not explain this unique occurrence, as it came "out of the blue," and I have never experienced anything like it before as a result of some pleasurable life event. It was definitely not triggered by me or anything I was doing or thinking.

Like the other two people I know who have had a similar occurrence, it was unique, unprecedented, not associated with or triggered by anything I was doing at the time, and unlike any other feeling or emotion I have ever had.

Where did this feeling come from and do spirits on the other side have this feeling continuously or sporadically? How does this feeling originate?

PRUDENCE ANN SMITH MD

Communicated through Penny 10/2/16

It was the intensified love and rapture that we can experience on the other side. We experience unprecedented feelings of love and bliss. Sensory experience, emotions, sounds, images, and colors are all more vivid and intense to a spirit not housed in the body.

Many are inexplicable in human terms, and spirits communicating are often at a loss for words to describe them.

We also dwell in an environment permeated by feelings of love and peace that cannot be compared with anything on earth. When we are free from the trappings of the flesh, more vivid and intense emotion and experience is common.

The feeling I gave you is a taste of what we can experience on the other side. It's like an intense jolt of electricity. Most spirits experience this and it's very similar between us. It is an overwhelming sense of exhilaration, peace, and love, a jubilant, exultant, ecstatic happiness, a pervasive climate, a feeling that is experienced by many spirits to a greater or lesser degree – tapping into the energy of the divine. It is open to all spirits who seek it and who wish to raise their vibration.

We can all experience it to some extent on our level of advancement. As we ascend, we experience more of these feelings of what you would call bliss or rapture. It is not always continually sustained, but it's part of what we are capable of expanding to and it is accessed by free will. In general, spirits in the afterlife experience peace and joy unknown on earth.

I gave you that feeling so you would know how we can feel in the afterlife and why, with greater joy, peace and love beyond those of our earthly experience, and without the wrongs and abuses permitted on earth, we are able to forgive others more easily and feel a divine type of love for all souls.

DIFFERENT ANSWERS

When there are different answers given to the same question, is it the medium or the spirit's fault?

Communicated through Penny 10/2/16

Any given Spirit can only give information commensurate with their level of awareness. Spirits, like people, are not all omniscient, and are subject to differing awareness and varying opinions.

No medium will be 100% accurate all of the time because information must be filtered through the human mind of the medium and can, as such, occasionally be distorted.

As mediums, if we work hard, we can achieve a 3% error rate rather than a 30%.

INFORMATION FROM PAST LIVES

How do we access the Akashic records to obtain information from our past lives that may help us overcome problems or deal with troubled relationships in our current life?

Communicated through Penny 10/2/16

We have strength and we have understanding. Most of the time we don't need to access our prior records.

If we have a very deep issue from a prior life that must be overcome in order to progress or that impedes our progression, we may be helped by the Akashic records in understanding and identifying or explaining that issue, and thereby, be able to address it or dismiss its power and hold on our current life accordingly.

Memories from past adverse events serve us to avoid certain behaviors in our future lives, but can also dominate our thoughts and inhibit or stymie us, and if so, awareness of their origin may help us in diminishing their power over us, and help us to address being paralyzed by such memories, enabling us to move forward in a positive manner, liberated from paralyzing fear.

PRUDENCE ANN SMITH MD

We request permission to access the information in our Akashic record or others' Akashic records. It is automatically conveyed to those whose task is to oversee the preservation of and access to the records. It often is through a formal prayer, but may also be individual.

There is an important factor. The asker must have a positive intention and will be limited to information that is helpful to him or herself or to the other recipient. The records are meant to be accessed only for a positive purpose, not for curiosity, and only those items or that data which will assist the individual is released to them.

When we pray we ask for wisdom and assistance in opening the records, and express appreciation for the permission of receiving and transmitting knowledge that will be of value to the progression and advancement of the receiving soul, whether we are the recipient or whether it is someone else on whose behalf we are seeking the information.

PRE-PLANNING TRAUMATIC EVENTS

If we planned to experience an adverse event at the hands of someone else on earth when we were planning our lives in the afterlife, why do we have to forgive one another in the afterlife?

Communicated through Penny 10/2/16

We are not perfect. When lives are planned to address a particular issue or flaw, we are meant to resolve issues or conflicts in the best manner possible and to learn from them. That doesn't mean we don't get hurt along the way or that we always complete our intended mission of resolving issues in the optimal manner.

Also, there is the element of unpredictable human free will and sometimes our actions and reactions were not planned, as we plan only a general path.

Therefore, as part of the learning experience, we must appreciate and be aware of the harm we have caused others, which, if not resolved on earth, must be resolved on the other side, complete with forgiveness, before souls can truly advance and say they have resolved a conflict or issue. In other words, they must "make things right", and a part of that is apology and resolution.

EVIL SPIRITS

Are there evil spirits?

Communicated through Penny 10/2/16

We are all capable of negative actions and thoughts or intentions. Whether or not a spirit is considered negative depends on their intent, whether they wish to harm by deliberate intent or harm by ignorance, accident, or lack of judgment. Some are influenced by passion or emotion of the circumstance. Others premeditate harm.

Some spirits are negative with malice or intent, and they may have been human. Negativity is part of what God's creation with free will permits, and, as such, nonhuman negative spirit entities can exist. Some are more powerful than others and they vary in intent.

God did not create negative souls. He created the possibility for negativity when he created free will. What humans call demons are nonhuman negative entities. They have the capability for becoming positive like negative human spirits, but do so only by choice. They are generally more powerful depending upon their will and level of development.

People can work at negativity or good and become more powerful or adept by practice and effort. Whatever we choose to work at we become.

If negative souls wish to become positive, they can. No soul is exempt from progress. It is their determination and is not imposed on them. Negative souls dwell on their own level of vibration. No soul is completely erased, obliterated, or destroyed.

INSPIRATION

How do you get answers for inspiration when you're in a miserable situation or when you suffer a severe loss?

Communicated through Harvey 10/4/16

Loss and negative events are opportunities to develop your ability to overcome adversity, and develop coping mechanisms. All negative events are to be looked at as teaching opportunities.

ADVICE

How do you get answers or inspiration when you're in a miserable situation or when you've suffered a severe loss?

Communicated through Penny 10/4/16

You need healing. Pray for strength. Pray for peace. Let your heart not be troubled. Remember that this too shall pass. Turn inward.

Accept healing from God. Forgive, banish bitterness, look with the soul and heart. Let go, pray, let God and Spirit. Deliver it into the hands of God. Trust.

RELATIONSHIP WITH GUIDES

Why do I not have an open, on-demand relationship with my guides?

Communicated through Penny 10/4/16

You have an open relationship when you are both communicating. You must sit in the power with dedication and ask. Remain open and seek.

When you are receiving an answer to your questions, you do have a two way relationship.

You must be serious and seek, and you will be answered. Keep an open heart. Ask for the gift of clairaudience. Gifts are there, but you must first seek and develop them.

It's a process as when you learn a skill. If you hear your guides answer when you're giving a reading, you can also hear their answers when they speak to you on your behalf.

You must trust. Seek and practice. All things in time if pursued.

HUMAN CRUELTY

Why can people live in the same environment and some turn out cruel and harmful, and others good? Even though we all learn and improve, are there core differences in our personalities that make some people more caring and kind and others colder and harmful?

Communicated through Harvey 10/16/16

Earth is not a utopia. We are exposed to good and bad during our lifetimes, and must choose the path to follow. We are not all equal in our morals. From a young age we make choices that chart our direction on earth – good or bad. Though we are taught the difference, we don't all choose the path that does not impact negativity on others. These traits are sometimes present at birth, and cannot be changed by proper upbringing.

NEGATIVE PERSONALITIES

Why are some spirits colder or more negative than others? Is it because they are less evolved, or because of an inherently different personality?

Communicated through Penny 10/16/16

We all have different strengths and weaknesses. Some people find one temptation more difficult to resist than others. Sometimes it takes a long time to overcome certain personality weaknesses. We find out about ourselves and work on our issues.

As we have different abilities and aptitudes, we also have different strengths and weaknesses, and carry them with us. We all have our own character and disposition and work on fine-tuning our negative aspects, our less desirable qualities.

They are not as relevant in the afterlife in terms of practice, but in terms of our wisdom, knowledge, and capability of creation, they are important for our development and perfecting ourselves to our highest potential - not to ameliorate our differences, but for each to eliminate the undesirable elements of our character, to eliminate self-centeredness, lack of love, until we display our best but different capacities, talents, and qualities, perfected in love.

ALIGNING KARMA

If people get into an endless cycle of vengeance, is there a way that karma can be balanced or be erased? How can we forgive heinous acts like murders and should the murderer be executed or in prison for life?

Communicated through Harvey on 12/16/16

When a loved one is lost due to the willful action of another, it may be impossible to forgive the perpetrator for their action that caused this pain and loss. The survivors may seek vengeance, but that will not fill the emptiness of their loved one's absence. Forgiveness may not be possible on earth, but may be possible in the afterlife.

Harvey's guides gave no answer regarding a judgment on whether capital punishment or life imprisonment is best.

KARMA AND PUNISHMENT

If people get into an endless cycle of vengeance, is there a way that karma can be balanced or erased? How can we forgive heinous acts like murders and should the murderer be executed or in prison for life?

Communicated through Penny on 12/16/16

Karma can be aligned by making new decisions and choices. We are able to do that by forgiving each other and opting not to continue the cycle. It comes from our own inner initiative, enlightenment, and courage to make new choices.

Only in a spiritual sense are we able to look beyond the human emotions. Only to the degree that we become more godlike or godly are we able to forgive acts of cruelty and violence. We aren't always able to forgive, but may not wish to return vengeance. We do not seek to return harm for harm. If we are able to look with the eyes of God we can forgive. If not, we can't. We don't have to seek harm for harm.

Those who commit murder are meant to be prevented from repeating their acts. They must be kept from harming others. If you are taking a life to prevent harm to others, that is a justifiable cause. If we enjoy killing, we are no different from the killer. We are not obligated to support murderers or torturers in luxury. It is up to people and society what they wish to do in terms of capital punishment or life imprisonment. The soul lives on.

RELATIONSHIPS IN THE AFTERLIFE

Why have some mediums said my mother and father are separated in the afterlife and others that they are joined at the hip? What is their relationship? Are they separated or together?

Communicated through Harvey 10/17/16

While it is not uncommon to be greeted in the afterlife by both parents who had a contentious relationship in life, they are not necessarily together after crossing. The pain of a poor relationship does not spill over, but they do not normally have a relationship after crossing over. It is not likely they would be "joined at the hip" after a poor relationship on earth. The medium was mistaken.

WISE ADVICE

Ask your guides to give you a piece of wise advice or something inspirational they have learned that they would give to someone they loved.

Communicated through Harvey 10/13/16

Enter into a relationship with no expectations or limitations. Keep an open mind and an open heart. Do not judge their motives or expectations by your own emotional needs. If love is to become a part of the relationship, it will be like a photograph, and develop over time.

INSPIRATIONAL ADVICE

What is a piece of wise advice or something inspirational that you have learned that you would give to someone you loved?

Communicated through Penny 10/13/16

When we start out life, we don't have any idea of what we're doing or where we're going. We change our ideas as we gain experience. We don't have the ability to change all of our circumstances as we would wish. We know what we want, but not always how to accomplish it. But one thing we must remember. We came here to learn, not to make things perfect. When we fall, we learn. When we stand, we learn. But only by falling do we learn to stand.

Forgive yourself your mistakes. Take the lesson with you and leave the regret behind. Follow your own truth and find out where it leads, because you will then never be untrue to yourself. Dreams begin in desires and we gain wisdom to accomplish them. Grow with your dreams and through them, and then one day you will live them.

WARNINGS FROM GUIDES

Recently I heard the story of a woman who had assistance and intervention from the other side that prevented her from being in the wrong place at the wrong time. The next day she read in the newspaper the account of another person who was where she ordinarily would have been the night before at the time she would have been there and was murdered. Why is it that some people are given messages and warnings from Spirit that protect them from danger, while others get harmed or killed, seemingly without guidance?

Communicated through Harvey on 1/23/17

Some people are open to spirit communications and heed warnings or feelings of impending danger. Others are not as fortunate and are in the wrong place at the wrong time, and are harmed.

Many do not have direct communication or knowledge of spirit guides.

Recently I heard the story of a woman who had assistance and intervention from the other side that prevented her from being in the wrong place at the wrong time. The next day she read in the newspaper the account of another person who was where she ordinarily would have been the night before at the time she would have been there and was murdered. Why is it that some people are given messages and warnings from spirit that protect them from danger, while others get harmed or killed, seemingly without guidance?

Communicated through Penny on 1/23/17

Many people are not aware when they are being given messages or influence because their belief systems do not support hunches. They may dismiss gut feelings as illogical, foolish, or unreasonable. Accidents and unplanned tragedies can occur.

Others may not be able to comprehend what is being given them because they are not spiritually "open", and do not accept such things as messages from spirit.

Free will always must be respected.

Spirit may intervene strongly if there is a great need for someone to be protected from the unforeseen accidents in life that are the product of free will and may prevent them from fulfilling an important life purpose or sidetrack their life's mission.

Some people have preplanned negative events or premature deaths written into their life contract.

Souls are given information as needed to accomplish important learning and teaching objectives in their lives.

Please note that in regard to the explanation above given from spirit, I, myself, have received guidance and messages from spirit. When I was young, my father came to me in a visitation in a dream, when I was fearful of an important life choice I was facing. He showed me the outcomes of the two alternatives in my dream, without influencing me in either direction. The choice was mine to make. A second time I got help from spirit, a dear friend of mine who was departed gave me a message through my grandmother, who was a medium, warning me of an impending dangerous situation of which I was not aware. Later, upon investigation, friends who knew a particular individual confirmed for me the danger I would have been in. This precisely matched my forewarning from spirit. Because of that forewarning, I avoided the danger.

DIVINE PURPOSE

Does God have a special purpose for each of us and to what extent can we set our own goals? As we ascend up the levels, can we remain an individual consciousness with our own unique will?

Communicated through Harvey 10/14/16

When we are sent to earth we are not sent with a life script. We are able to use free will from the time of birth. We are influenced by our surroundings, exposures, and our ego and personal drive and aspirations.

As we ascend in the afterlife, we retain some of our former identities, but they are less important as we grow closer to Source. We do retain some of our former consciousness, but free will is not as important.

DIVINE PURPOSE AND FREE WILL

Does God have a special purpose for each of us and to what extent can we set our own goals? As we ascend up the levels can we remain an individual consciousness with our own unique will?

Communicated through Penny 10/14/16

There are general spiritual laws we observe on the other side. Our mandate is not to harm others and we are much freer because we do not dwell in an environment that permits harm. With free will we have options in directing our own path but work in partnership with the divine and have freedom within our intent. We are not given demands, but rather expectations. Our path is ours to direct within the divine framework and we have plans we are intended to fulfill.

We have free will as long as we choose to exist in separate consciousness. We are a thinking entity with choice, will, and direction. That is not taken from us as long as we choose to maintain it. God does not forcibly retract our prerogative. If we wish to remain a separate entity we can.

CREATION OF SOULS

Why did God create individual souls?

Communicated through Penny 10/15/16

We are designed to be co-creators with God. God is a loving, creative, intelligent energy. We are energy with intelligence. That implies a purposeful direction of that energy. We are meant to use our energy responsibly. We are learning to co-create in love and with positive direction.

Our volition entails free will and we are in an apprenticeship to learn to co-create in wisdom and love with our Creator. As such, our free will permits negative and positive direction of our energy. We are in training for the development of our creative energy to be used in the pursuit of positive outcomes in concert with our Creator as co-creators.

As God is energy with intelligent direction, God creates, directs, and seeks other energies in love as a spirit, as we do other spirits in love to interact, create, and exist within loving relationships and partnerships in creation. Do we who also are spirits want children, families and relationships? As the greatest Spirit, our Source, it is understandable that God would wish to have other consciousness, other spirits with whom to interact. What is love for if there is no one to love? Ask yourself as you, too, are a spirit. The answers are within you.

Does God demand love, allegiance or praise? God has given us free will of choice. God doesn't demand love from us. God is worthy of love. Do we want someone to praise us out of force? That type of recognition would not be from real appreciation or love. We want someone to appreciate us because they love us for who we are.

ORIGIN OF GOD

What is the origin of God and existence, or have God and existence always been?

Communicated through Penny 10/15/16

As I partake of the Spirit of God and it is the Spirit of God within me that gives me life, and the Spirit of God in all souls, all creatures, that animates them, God's origin is also my origin. We maintain separate consciousness from God and separate will, only by God's will. God gives us a foretaste of heaven in his spirit.

God's presence is the best of all possible choices, the perfection of desire and purpose based on the principles of love, forgiveness, peace, joy, and wisdom.

God is our origin and our origin is in God. Spirit is eternal backwards and forwards. Spirit will always be and always was. Creation is a continual unending act that had no finite inception. It is continual inception of endless creation, endless becoming, and endless dynamic change orchestrated by intelligent energy, dynamic love, power with purpose acting upon its surroundings.

The universe itself is alive, the product of God, an unending production, of a Spirit that is energy with awareness, consciousness with direction, manifestation based upon the foundation of love.

God is the great I am who was, is, and always will be, without beginning, without end.

THE NATURE OF GOD

What is the origin of God? Has God always existed or was God created? What do you know of God?

Communicated through Harvey 10/23/16

God has existed before time, and is the energy source that fuels all existence. All energy that guides the universe has its existence from God. All life forces came from God's energy. God is a loving spirit and forgives our failures.

PART II

REFLECTIONS ON SPIRIT

WHO SAYS UNDERSTANDING IS EASY?

For many years after I embarked on the spiritual pathway consciously, I struggled with resolution of issues in my own life, what my lessons were, why certain bad things happened to me, what I did right or wrong, how I could have possibly prevented things, what better choices would have been, and how other people would have responded if I had made different choices.

Before I could move forward, I had to understand the facts, why it happened the way it did and what I could have done differently – the "what if's". Only then with that insight could I make peace with the past, forgive myself and others, and move forward.

Part of my quest was to understand the afterlife. I came from there, but my memories have been wiped clean. Only vague convictions in my heart remained. Just as some people say that the old-fashioned view of heaven as all of us flying around with wings playing harps all day is a fantasy, I also believe that some of the notions currently popular - of instant, complete forgiveness between souls, of instant perfection of souls upon death, of obliteration of personal love and feelings for each other as individual souls, to be replaced by a generic equal love for all souls regardless of who they are, or the idea that we lose all personal identity and become a great sludge or clone, are distorted ideas.

Do I believe in forgiveness? Absolutely. Do I believe in prayer and perfection? Yes. But I believe we work at forgiveness. I believe that we address issues and work out solutions. I believe that we work gradually toward perfection over many lifetimes and levels in the afterlife. I believe we retain individual identity of who we are and were in our past lives and that we relate to souls differently. I believe that we have closer, deeper loves for some souls than for others and that some we choose as our companions, and others we see little of or separate from. I believe that as souls we each have and make individual choices that are right for us regarding these issues. I believe that souls, although not placed in situations of negativity in the afterlife, still have a capacity for anger or sadness.

Kelvin Cruickshank, in his book, *"Finding the Path"*, describes some souls who died traumatically and unexpectedly and don't know they're dead, some who didn't want to die, some who are unable to move forward due to the violent manner in which they died, and some who are fearful of judgment or have unfinished business. He also describes some souls who have harmed others deeply in their earth lives, and who remain in denial about the damage they have done, yet are on the other side and have moved to the light. Every case appears different. Apparently some souls take time to acknowledge their faults and the pain they have caused others, some take time to heal from their injuries, and some take time to forgive one another and make peace.

I have a cousin in the afterlife who died young, and communicated to me that it took time and effort for her to forgive a close relative who had injured her deeply, but that with work, she was able to forgive him and resolve the issues between them.

I do believe that there is a higher, more godly type of humanitarian love and helpfulness in the afterlife, where souls aid each other. But I also believe there are different levels of development or advancement, with some souls remaining negative for a shorter or longer period of time, entailing healing and learning.

I feel that there are many different aspects to the afterlife with very different choices, and that souls gravitate to other like-minded souls and to environments that are uniquely suitable for them.

I know that souls can become upset, agitated, annoyed, and sad. I know that there remains some drama in the afterlife, and some earthly problems or situations can bleed over. Some issues take time to resolve.

I know that the afterlife is part of an upward climb, not geographically, but spiritually. It is both work and leisure and is a place where we, so to speak, judge ourselves, as we end up in a place that is commensurate with the quality of the life we led.

It can also be the place of dreams come true for those who have attempted to lead kind, loving, and unselfish lives. I am told that we can have our dreams come true, as long as they do not entail harm to others.

Some claim to have visited the afterlife and have reported some common and some different experiences, but those who have not experienced a negative environment describe astounding beauty, peace and general love.

My guide states that there's nothing like it. "It's different from earth life. It's better. No worries, no upsets, no cares, no people hurting you, no crime, no anger, no sickness or pain. It's like having a vacation in a beautiful spot where nothing goes wrong. No one struggles for a living. No sickness or pain. No unhappy circumstances. We don't have the earthly drives or miss the earthly needs. We have a different mindset.

We can create the experience of eating, but not with the physical apparatus of earth. It's like a mind game.

It's an illusion created by the mind. Hallucinations on earth feel real to the hallucinator, don't they? You could never convince those who undergo hallucinations that the things that they are feeling and seeing are not real. Well, this is similar. You create your reality with your thoughts. You won't miss sex if you want it. You can create the sensations and feelings of sex as well as you can on earth. You create the reality with the thought, and the feelings are there, the sensations are there, the apprehension is there.

We create that reality, that situation, with our intentions and thoughts. The experience is created when you create it with your thoughts and you experience it in such a manner that it is real to you. We'll be able to feel each other exactly as we would have on earth. The sensations, although not mediated in the same manner, will be received by our minds and thoughts in the same manner and feel identical to what we would have felt and experienced on earth.

What we experience is the product of our own creation and experiences with co-creators. In that manner Heaven becomes the place of our dreams. We can experience those things dearest to us as long as we are not harming others. We have greater peace, love, joy, forgiveness, and acceptance, lacking all the negativity of earth. Heaven is a blissful place where you are not harmed, where harmony exists, a loving environment free of negativity, and a place in which fulfillment and dreams are realized. That is the Heaven I know. There is nothing anyone could imagine that could be better than this. When you come here, you will experience what you desire the most."

COMMUNICATING WITH SPIRIT

Kelvin Cruickshank, a New Zealand psychic medium who gained fame on the television series "Sensing Murder" as a psychic detective helping to solve cold cases, describes entering the high velocity vibrational state of spirit while still remaining on the physical plane in order to communicate, invoking a sort of dual citizenship, having a foot in each world.

Through his communications he is able to hear the dead person's story, often with details of names, addresses, birth, family, life story, lessons, and death. The deceased spirit can communicate these details to us and is aware of our thoughts, as well as what is happening in our lives. He is even able to see their life story like a video clip in the Akashic records, the etheric record that contains information on each spirit's lifetimes.

Not only can spirits communicate auditorily through clairaudience, impart feelings through clairsentience, and visions through clairvoyance, they can at times communicate smells or tastes. Some develop the ability to affect our physical environment by moving objects, making sounds, speaking, or showing themselves as apparitions. Spirits can touch us. Spirits can even in effect "yell at you" or re-create all of the emotions they had in their earth lives, including the physical feelings they had at their death.

We connect soul to soul and, as Kelvin Cruickshank puts it, experience spirit in a multi-sensory fashion, drawing upon our own internal databank of experiences, including seeing, hearing, feeling, and smelling through spirit — so to speak, "feeling the vibe".

FWH Myers, paranormal researcher, communicating through medium Geraldine Cummins, states that love, affection, and intense interest help to bridge the gap.

Arthur Findlay college mediums and tutors, Chris Drew and Andy Byng, emphasize the important role of mediums in telling the story by taking on the spirit's memories of circumstances, events, emotions, and physical feelings. The medium takes on the persona of the spirit, blending with that spirit temporarily.

THE SERVICE OF MEDIUMSHIP

My guide channels,

"Mediumship is meant to bring people together, to provide comfort, to inspire direction, to resolve issues, to provide awareness, to impart lessons, to encourage forgiveness, to enhance awareness, to inspire growth, and to confirm and share love.

Spirits come through for all these reasons and continue to take part in the lives of those they love. Love and its many manifestations is the intended and proper driving force.

Creative endeavor, constructive thought, benevolent action, positive design, conferring blessings, disseminating knowledge, acting for the good, for the mutual welfare and benefit of all, is our mission.

We are engaged in a stewardship, an apprenticeship, and given a pallet of colors, a set of tools, a dictionary of words, a cache of melodies, inspired by spirit to make new songs, to paint new portraits, to craft new masterpieces all designed in the framework of love, a testimony to the truth in our soul.

We should seek to be a mirror where light is reflected, not a black hole where light is sucked in and absorbed or effaced. We are meant to transform all situations to good, to make that which is positive from that which is negative.

Hand to the plow, take what you were given and do not let your talents lie fallow, but develop them, make them fertile, hone them, utilize them, grow them, demonstrate the spiritual principles through physical acts and deeds. Make yours a composition of light, one that you will be proud to put your signature upon, one that you will be proud to display and share, one that will produce wonder and happiness in all that see it."

CHARMED LIVES?

You would think that mediums, knowing that there is an afterlife and getting inspiration from the other side, would lead charmed lives. Not so. I have friends who are mediums whose lives are every bit as bad as anyone else's, including family disputes, financial woes, trouble with children, physical health issues, divorce, loneliness, etcetera.

In fact, I begin to see an emerging pattern, and I have theorized that mediums on the whole often have difficult, problematic lives. I think this is because they have chosen a profession that requires empathy with many souls' different issues, and in order to understand those issues and help people, mediums must experience similar problems and traumatic events.

Nothing is as vivid as having the experience yourself. Until we know what it is like to bear a child, we can only guess at the experience. Guides can only effectively guide someone if they have successfully navigated through the same type of experience.

Would you choose someone to guide you through the Alaskan wilderness who had never been there? When mediums suffer so much trauma, I think they are in preparation for a life of service, enabling them to gain the wisdom needed to relate to and help others.

EMPATHS, SENSITIVES, AND PECULIAR VIEWS OF THE AFTERLIFE

One aspect of opening up as a medium that can be confusing or distressing is the increased openness or sensitivity that one needs to develop for connection with the spirit world.

This increased sensitivity not only opens you up to clearer connection and messages from Spirit, but also to increased sensitivity to the energies and feelings of other people around you. In other words, as a sensitive, you will likely be more aware of or open to the emotions of other people. You may wonder why you are experiencing a certain sensation or mood. It is easier to incorporate others' moods, experience them, and perhaps even feel they are your own.

It is important to learn to set boundaries, not only in regard to the times of your communication so that you aren't always "working" and burn out, and in terms of the vibration of the spirits you allow into your space, so that you don't allow yourself to be influenced by negative spirits, but also in terms of defining your own feelings, attitudes, and opinions, so that you don't absorb those of others around you, confusing them with your own.

For a while, I would be troubled by some things that I read, were expressed by others, or were conveyed on a TV program. This was particularly so when the attitudes were very opposed to or contradictory to my own formerly held beliefs. It was easy to start second-guessing myself.

After I pondered these issues and had a great advisory session with my guide, I began to have more faith in my own convictions, my "truth", my communications with the other side, and to be less swayed by others' opinions and energies.

Also, I have been exposed to many different opinions of those I have associated with or discussed issues with. One subject which has come up several times is the belief some people have that souls lose their individual connections in the afterlife with those they have loved in life and simply have a generic equal love for all souls, whether they are a lost beloved child or a serial killer who raped and murdered their child. According to those who express such beliefs, all ex-husbands and wives are blissfully together no matter how horrible the relationship in life, and no one has any special bond with anyone else.

I do not believe either of these ideas for a second. Often, on closer inspection, I have found that some of those who expound such beliefs do not display or demonstrate their own convictions in their personal lives. One person who had previously made such comments went on to have a very bitter and acrimonious divorce with her husband. Oops. What happened to the equal blissful love with all ex-partners that she passionately lectured me on?

Another had been divorced, with no lasting love relationship or partnership, yet that person was an authority on the impartial generic love on the other side, with no personal preferences or special bonds and connections - perhaps because she never had one. Thank God for my own truth.

I would not want their truth, not want their conception of Heaven, any more than they would want mine. God bless my grandmother, who said, "Each to his own". I'll live in my own preferences, thank you. Find your own truth. Don't let me or anyone else define yours.

None of us know the whole truth until we get there. We only get more or less objective/subjective glimpses. But unless we are automatically converted to automatons or robots by God when we die, then people will continue to have individual preferences and personalities.

Another concept that strikes me oddly is the idea I have heard from several mediums that we all lose our individuality on the other side, and immediately the picture of "Stepford wives" or clones came into my mind.

How many different ways of living and cultures exist on earth? Would we all be happy living off the grid in the Alaskan wilderness or in a penthouse in Manhattan? Would we all be happy with multiple wives, polygamy, or being spinsters or bachelors and living alone? Would everyone be happy being a surgeon, a test pilot, a mortician, or a nuclear scientist? Of course not. Take away individuality and we cease to be who we are. Why go to all the trouble of being born and living a turbulent earth life, why learn lessons if we no longer are an individual on the other side? What are the lessons for if there's no remnant of our individuality or progress?

In fact, why go through the adversity of learning difficult lessons if we are instantly perfected or lose our identity to become someone else when we die? That would be futile or redundant.

What's the point of loving at all or living in the first place if all the relationships we've built up are ameliorated or negated? The love we've built up with people over a lifetime – kids, parents, spouses, friends? Gone? Insignificant? No bonds left? Just an altruistic, generic, equanimous impersonal love for all? I'm not knocking a humanitarian, godly, non-judgmental, altruistic love. It's very important to have kindness, helpfulness and charity toward all. But if the individual love bonds I have been blessed with in my life all disappear when I hit the other side, well, that's more like Hell to me than Heaven. Why would God want to give us something so beautiful to take it away? That's cruel. Even crueler than the murderers on earth. How would you feel if the human child, parent, husband, wife, brother or sister you love were taken from you by a murderer? That's a temporary devastating physical loss, and many say their lives are never the same. What if God did that on the other side and it were a permanent spiritual loss of those we have loved?

No, thanks, I do not want to become a cloned, generic soul with no personal identity with a non-descript impersonal love for all other souls equally, with no special feelings for anyone, no remembrance of the love I had for those dear to me, and no individuality left. Pardon the pun, but that's a fate worse than death to me, because at that point "I" will have been annihilated along with all the relationships and deep loves I have ever had. Continuing life like that? Not worth it. I wouldn't even call it life.

SOULS WHO ACT IN GOOD OR EVIL

I have always wondered why some people are more negative and others more positive in their behavior. Are some souls inherently bad, are they just unlearned, or do we all have personality differences that predispose us to selfishness or kindness, empathy or cruelty?

None of us is perfect. We all have flaws, but not the same flaws. Some have more destructive flaws than others. We are a combination of our own unique identity and personality, modified and developed by the experiences we undergo.

Some people appear inherently less sensitive or caring than others. Feelings may vary, but it is up to us how we choose to develop what we have.

God did not create "bad" souls. People create "bad" – ignorant or unlearned people, as we have free will.

Why some people more readily choose bad or don't seem to have a conscience or care for other people is unclear. Attempting to attribute this entirely to environment isn't sufficient because some people exposed to the same environment are destructive, while others are productive. And what about negative nonhuman entities who can't blame their actions on persecution from human life? Why or how did they get negative?

No one can explain why negative entities are negative. They don't have to contend with negative human experiences and can't blame their behavior on persecution or mistreatment.

Pride, ego, selfishness, and lack of empathy or concern for others are traits that are not completely understood. There certainly is a spectrum of such traits in human form, but also in spiritual essence.

Our spirit is comprised of conscious intelligence like God's, but having free will necessitates that we can choose good or evil, or a combination of both.

Why some choose evil is a mystery. As humans, we all have weaknesses, and if we haven't encountered certain lessons yet or are "ignorant", so to speak, we are disposed to act less conscientiously or make more mistakes. These souls are undeveloped or uninformed, but what of those who are deliberately malicious, who appear to enjoy harming others? Perhaps they have an essence or unique disposition, quality, or nature that makes them less empathetic, less giving, less caring.

Even those who seem more spiritually evolved appear to have different dispositions. Even in the same environment, all people have different natures and act differently. There is a unique soul quality and individuality, acted upon by environment. Some describe "hard" and "soft" souls, those who are merciful and caring or compassionate, and others who are cold, self-centered, and malicious. The old nature or nurture argument comes to mind. We each have different predispositions, which are then influenced by our circumstances and environment.

We each have an inherent nature that is shaped by what we undergo. Just think of yourself and how alike or different you are and your reactions are, to others in your environment, to those you know well or who are close to you. The variety of options and behavior is amazing. Would you enjoy torturing or killing animals and people as some do? We can't understand the mentality of those who do so, as they can't understand ours.

The ultimate destiny of such souls and how long they remain negative is beyond our awareness. The ability to change is in their hands, and must be elected by them, if at all.

In the afterlife, I believe that the negative souls cannot act upon their desires, and that those who are positive are protected from negative influences and intentions, whereas on earth we all coexist and are prey to the behavior of others. As humans, we must protect ourselves physically and spiritually from those who would desire to harm us.

Although the option to change is available to all, the will to change must originate within.

Some of these same principles are described in the Bible, which refers to "spiritual wickedness in high places", and that we should put on our spiritual armor for protection.

PRUDENCE ANN SMITH MD

Whether or not one believes in the Bible or accepts it literally if they do, the principles of spiritual choice, the ability to harm or help others, to walk in darkness or light, are evidenced all around us, and certainly can't be denied when they affect us personally. Choices are ours to walk in the light or darkness.

WHAT IS THE TRUTH? NEGATIVE AND POSITIVE SOULS

What are we like when we die? Do negative souls remain negative and positive, positive?

Can negative souls influence us?

As not one person on earth has all the truth, not one medium has all the truth. No two human beings agree on every single point - the same with mediums. Many of their viewpoints are individual, sometimes influenced by culture, personality differences, and personal experiences.

When souls die, I am told that they remain basically the same and work to change. Seeing the bigger picture and undergoing the life review can change their perception and feelings toward how they acted on earth, but yet they remain a distinct individual with unique personality traits and characteristics. As with people on earth, some can change and evolve more quickly, and others are more set in their ways and resist change longer.

They are the people we knew with expanded consciousness, no more need for a particular age, gender, or set of cultural or social attributes. I am told we become aware of our past identities and lives and have greater awareness as souls than we had on earth. We become less tied to our previous specific identity as we progress in the afterlife, but at least initially we are the same person we were, changed somewhat by the lessons we learned and our new knowledge.

In the words of my guide, "I am the same person I was, just a little bit kinder, more caring, and loving."

It is apparent that we are protected to an extent by those who love us, either by lost love ones we knew on earth or those we knew on the other side. Not all souls are loving. Some are positive and helpful, and some very negative, dark, low vibration energies.

Spirits can influence us both positively and negatively. That is why it is so important to set boundaries and ask for spiritual protection. I personally know a kind, intelligent, loving medium who had a negative spirit attempt to create havoc in her home, and several other reputable mediums I know have experienced scratches and pejorative remarks from spirits when they were attempting to assist people experiencing hauntings. Some no longer wish to expose themselves to that kind of work, and have expressed the importance of protecting themselves spiritually with prayer and assistance from their guides, loved ones, and angels when they communicate with the spiritual realm. Others set the intention of working only at the vibration of love, barring out those who have malicious intent.

I had been having some terrible nightmares a while ago and I couldn't understand why. They involved reliving traumatic experiences I had had earlier, but progressed beyond that into the present. I was perplexed. Did my guides give those dreams to me for learning? They said no. Was I just processing former negative experiences as a psychologist friend of mine suggested? Were negative events just being replayed?

I also noticed that sometimes statements, thoughts, or comments would "pop into my mind ", that were negative or insulting, totally uncharacteristic of me, and things that I would never have said before. These were definitely nothing I felt or believed. I only realized what was happening when I had a dream with a very clear instruction to kill myself. I knew that wasn't from my guides or me and all of a sudden I had insight. The statement was clear as day and did not come from my own mind. I knew it came from someone in spirit. Since I had spiritually opened up, I could hear negative spirits as well as positive. Negative spirits or entities were capable of talking to me and attempting to influence me.

I realized I had always asked for spiritual protection before spirit circle, but not in my personal life. As I became more sensitive, I was aware of both negative and positive spirits. I know that negative spirits and entities exist. I have no doubt whatsoever. They exist in this world as well as after death in the spirit realm.

At that moment , I recognized the need to pray for protection and set boundaries, barring out negative souls, entities, and thoughts from life and invoking the white light of God's protection over myself, loved ones, and home.

Now I seldom have negative dreams.

On a weekend that I was unavailable, one of the individuals in our Skype spirit circle was involved in helping another member's friend to transition over. That evening and the next day my friend from the circle called me to tell me her mood was atypical and she had been experiencing unusual negativity, when she realized that during the transition at the spirit circle while she was open to the other side she had been exposed to a negative spirit with lower vibrational energy who had decided to hang around and was influencing her. After a cleansing and prayer she was able to rid herself of the "hanger-on". In this same manner, occasionally someone has reported coming back from a near death experience with a spirit from one of the lower vibrational levels tagging along, and has to have a cleansing and crossing ceremony to remove them.

There are negative people, souls, and entities. We need to exercise care to not let them in to harm and influence us. They, like people with negative agendas, never give up completely, and as long as we are alive on the earth, must seek protection from them as we would from predators in the flesh.

Weakness, illness, unawareness, substance-abuse, Satanic worship, and other dark practices allow them in. Spiritual protection is paramount.

Answers from the Afterlife

Each of us needs to find our own truth. Never accept what someone else says is right for you. We must each find our own faith, our own higher truth, our own inner answers.

In his book, *"Finding the Path"*, Kelvin Cruikshank states, "Those who have passed over find their heaven where they set themselves free." One person's heaven is not necessarily another's. One doesn't fit all. We each find our own.

I have not been informed that communicating with the dead, per se, is in itself bad. I have been told that communicating with bad intentions or with negative souls is bad and harmful.

Many mediums indicate that they are happy and inspired by their contact with the spirit world, and consider it a privilege to receive and give positive and healing messages. The idea that our loved ones continue to live, have peace, and remain connected with us and present in our lives, is very healing for those who have suffered traumatic grief. Mediums are convinced through this communication that those we love are not dead. They have merely made a change or transition. They are the same souls that they were when they were living here with us on earth.

Such mediums, who operate at the vibration of love, indicate that it is only bad to talk with the dead when our own intentions are negative or bad, or when we fail to place adequate protection around ourselves and others, putting ourselves and others at risk of negative communication, or attack. Numerous mediums I have heard indicate that when our intention is to understand, to learn, to grow, and to help ourselves and others, we will encounter good communications. When things are done in the spirit of love they will have a good outcome. Just as in the physical realm we draw experiences to us that match our intentions, so in the spiritual realm we attract what we wish for. I personally know that I am communicating with the spirit world and have had many absolute personal proofs throughout the years. Each person must seek or judge this for himself or herself if they so desire.

RETENTION OF IDENTITY

I have been told that we remain the individuals we are when we cross over to the other side and that our personalities remain intact, except for the changes we embrace as a result of our life lessons and our life reviews, in which we see the impact of our own actions and those of others. Those changes include examining and recognizing our own errors, and attempting to become a little bit better, a little more caring.

I have heard many times through other mediums, as well as others who have made a study of the paranormal their life's pursuit, that spirits' personalities do not change or improve when they die. Personalities remain as they were, and negative souls can remain negative when they die, working hard to change that negativity and their own negative personality characteristics.

One of these substantiating comments came to a relative of mine in a dream he had of a dear friend communicating with him. That friend, who had committed some very harmful acts towards others in his lifetime, indicated that he was not in a good place, but that soon he would be able to get to a little better place not far away. It was such an emotional dream or visitation, that my relative woke up emotionally distraught and crying.

If we lost our identity when we crossed over, we would just be cookie cutter clones, ticky-tacky souls, all the same. What would be the purpose of loving anyone if they turned into someone else when they died, or if there were no longer any difference between us? Our thoughts and individuality, our personalities would be annihilated. What would be the purpose of learning if we weren't even the same person? Why would there be a need for lower or negative levels if we were all instantly perfected when we crossed over?

I once read comments from a medium who said we are just playing roles here, that we change into someone else when we die, without our current flaws or faults. Then murderers and serial killers would be no different from humanitarians or religious figures. No moral distinctions would exist. If all we are doing is playing roles, putting on costumes and adopting fake personas, why bother coming to earth in the first place? If we are just "play acting" and not the person we think we are, there would be no need for us to learn and progress, no need to develop or to ascend levels in the afterlife. There would be no need for a life review or to forgive one another. What would the need for learning be if we aren't even the same individuals when we cross over, if we're just all perfect carbon copies? Jeffrey Dahmer would be synonymous with Jesus or Genghis Kahn with Ghandi.

If we are all just fakes, why do spirits who have interacted with us in a negative way, such as an abusive parent, feel the need to come through and apologize to us for the way they acted? The idea that we are all just playing roles and change into different and improved people automatically when we die negates the need for lessons, levels, learning, progression, and spiritual development.

Answers from the Afterlife

"Claude's Book" states that personality is the child of spirit and body, and never lost.

Gretchen Vogel communicates that the essential nature of the deceased does not change just because they don't have a physical body.

Kelvin Cruickshank says that spirits' personalities remain intact, and they can relive their experiences with the emotions. He also comments that in death we are restored to our peak energy. While on earth our physical conditions may have limited us, after death the soul regains full expression.

Raymond, communicating to Sir Oliver Lodge, indicates that we retain affinities, repulsions, personality, interests, and idiosyncrasies.

Charlotte Dresser communicates that spirit is substantial, more substantial than the material world.

SPIRIT SENSES

How do spirits experience the familiar sensations of touch, sight, hearing, taste, smell and emotion?

My guide explains, "We can simulate all forms of emotion, physical feeling, touch, hearing, images, smell, and taste with our minds and thoughts and reproduce these. That is how spirits impart those sensations to mediums. The medium feels them as though they were experiencing them through their physical sensory apparatus, but in actuality they are being conveyed through the mind directly, in the same manner by which those in spirit convey and receive sensation, information, and feelings.

We can simulate them in such a way that we experience them just as though they were perceived by the physical body. They will feel the same and real to us, but are relayed in a different manner, not through the senses, but through the mind, spirit, and spirit senses. Although the means, the mechanism may be different, the end or outcome, the apprehension, is the same. The perception and feelings are the same.

That is how communication is accomplished in Spirit. That is how spirits can reproduce or relive the sensations of physical experience. They are stored in the mind and can be simulated at will. The simulation, although not created through a network of physical nerves, creates the same effect. In the physical our sensory cells and neural cells only gather data from our environment and convey it to the brain, which interprets it and allows us to experience and perceive, feel and see the information coming in to us and to interpret or experience it.

When that information comes directly to us in spirit, the result is the same. We in a sense create or re-create the experience we wish and actually relive it, feeling and sensing the same outcome that we would have had in the physical, but without the intervening physical sensory mechanism. Therefore the experience will be identical in feeling to the one we would have had on earth. It is just created in a different way."

The spirit experiencing it will feel it as being as real as the earthly experience. The feelings and sensations are completely reproducible. That is why spirits say they can eat in spirit and why they create many things with their minds. Whatever the building blocks, chemicals, or elements, substance or ether of the spirit world, for lack of a better word, the spirit world feels as real and "solid" to those who inhabit it as our world does to us.

I have seen several mediums who have been given clairsentient sensations by spirits, and they felt the same physical sensations as those spirits did at the time of their death. The sensations were so real and so intense that the mediums had to ask the spirits to stop.

The perceptions and sensations are just as real. We are told that the spirit world is the real one and the physical world the illusion – not an illusion in the sense that it doesn't exist, but in the sense that it is a partial, temporary reality, designed for us to learn lessons without the idyllic atmosphere of a dimension run by God, but rather an environment in which good and evil, negative and positive are permitted to exist simultaneously, side by side, so that we as souls with free will learn to choose the good, the positive, over the negative, by experiencing the consequences of negative experiences to ourselves and others.

Charlotte Dresser indicates that souls have the spiritual equivalent of physical sensations analogous to the mortal ones, but not gained through the mortal organs. Spirit can give sensation as perfectly as nerves. Thought often expresses the emotion.

Anthony Borgia's book states that souls are able to see, hear, and touch one another on their own plane and feel as solid to one another as they did on earth. As each successive dimension or plane is of a higher or finer vibration, although not appreciated or seen to those on a lower level, spirits appear solid to those inhabiting their level.

In *"Claude's Book"*, the author states that spirits directly feel and sense one another. They practice clairvoyance and communicate through feeling. They can also "speak" through words if they wish. Many who first undergo the change called death continue to desire to see one another and use words as they used to.

Kelvin Cruickshank describes the soul to soul connection. He states that our experience as spirits is multi-sensory and we can feel, see, hear, smell, and touch through spirit. That is how mediums get the story, feel the vibe.

Gretchen Vogel communicates that spirits still get the same information as we do when light strikes the optic nerves and the chemical reaction transmits that information to the brain, but the information comes directly into the mind of the spirit and is as accurate as if gained through the physical senses.

The spirit group Silver, communicating through another medium, states that our senses are a relay system developed to bring in information so that we have awareness and can process thoughts. The senses are a vehicle for our experience. We no longer need that mediator in spirit, but nevertheless can experience and have available to us all of those same sensations that were a vital part of our awareness and satisfaction.

Gretchen Vogel indicates that some of the emotions and sensory expressions are not felt as vividly after we ascend levels in the afterlife.

SPIRIT APPEARANCE

My guide states, "I was not my body. I was a consciousness inside and directing the body. The body was a vehicle for sensory input and expression. Now I have a form, a body, so to speak, that is different from the material body, and its form and appearance are changeable and controlled by thought. It is not just a projected thought form or hologram but an actual body with a different form and substance from the earthly body.

Our outward form is the replica of our inner vision. We become the product of our own thoughts. We manifest with our will and set intentions, both in regard to ourselves and our surroundings."

I have been told that spirits can assume the appearance they had on earth or change their malleable "spirit body" into an orb, a mist, a humanoid or non-humanoid form.

Regarding the spirit body, Anthony Borgia's book states, we have etheric bodies which are a replica of our old physical form, and can see, hear, and touch one another. We feel solid to each other, and if we reside in a spirit body, which has form and substance, we can be seen by those inhabiting the same level of vibration.

"Claude's Book" states that we have solid bodies controlled by our thoughts, which in our conditions, are solid to us as yours are to you, but which, insofar as they are matter, are completely under the control of mind.

Gretchen Vogel's book says that the dead clothe themselves with the memory of their prior body at whatever age is desired, through the projection of their mind. They look solid and feel real to each other. In other words, they create their own experience and can change their age or appearance at will.

Charlotte Dresser states that spirits can assume the outline of material form and change their appearance with their thought.

Kelvin Cruickshank states that spirits can look any way they want.

Shanna Spalding St. Clair channels, we inhabit different energy sheaths. "We are light inhabiting form. We transmute the outward manifestation of our existence in conformity to the need for karmic progression through successive incarnations, maintaining form until we reunite with Source."

The medium, L, states that we can go back-and-forth between energetic form and body, with conditions in the lower planes more earthlike. We can assume a more physical type of form if we wish, usually for comfort or contact with loved ones for the purpose of touch, speech, etc. There are choices. There is everything. You do have a unique appearance on the other side separate from your incarnations, but can change that appearance to something you like better if so desired.

As I have wondered how spirits recognize each other on the other side if they can change their appearance or don't necessarily have to maintain a humanoid form, a reading I got from a friend who is a medium helped me to understand. She stated that she recognizes the energy of different spirits when they come through, as she recognized the energy of one of my deceased relatives.

From my understanding, it is recognition of their essence, thought patterns, and personality. This is said with the caveat that a spirit can disguise their typical energy, that is, withhold the communication of their typical energy in a reading so that they can transmit new information about themselves through a medium who may have brought them through before, in an unbiased manner. They do this so that the medium will not be prejudiced in their reading by what they already know about that spirit.

PLANNING REINCARNATIONS

I have been told that in the afterlife we, as soul groups, write our own story, plan our own lessons and incarnation to provide the soul learning we need. We, as a group, and individually, with assistance and input from more advanced spiritual advisors, in essence, write our own script.

This has been borne out in many comments I have heard through other mediums that we plan the challenges we need to overcome in order to grow when we're on earth. There is a master plan that we, ourselves, have laid out before we come to earth. That is why some mediums state that certain tragic events in life and deaths cannot be prevented or stopped. They are part of that person's chosen learning experience that they must go through. That is why some events which are known beforehand cannot be changed or altered. If a tragedy is not part of a person's path, then there may be a choice. This is also evident in those who have had near death experiences. Some state that they are not given choices but must return to earth and others have been given choices to return or remain in the afterlife. It has been stated that we have a plan or mission for this life which we worked out with our Creator before we came here to the physical plane. Our objective in the physical life is discovering what our mission is and accomplishing our preplanned learning objective.

When it comes to planning incarnations, in order to have free will, they must not be forced or planned by God without any input from us. On the other hand they must be planned in conjunction with more knowledgeable spiritual advisors. Otherwise there would be infinite choices and chaos. Of the countless numbers of choices in the universe, how could we look at them all to decide which we wanted? What if others wanted that same choice? Who would decide who got it? Or would the limitless number of souls be brawling up in Heaven to try to see who gets it? Images of the Jerry Springer show flood my mind. What would happen to the need for multiple souls in a soul group to work out their lessons together so they all benefit from a reincarnation and so that they aren't just drones to fulfill the purposes of others? That would necessarily limit our choices.

So there must be choices to preserve free will, but a finite number of choices to prevent chaos and to ensure the benefit of all parties involved in a reincarnation. Also, if life is a school and we are learning, there must be some teachers or guidance. Therefore, there must be advisory input from those who are more advanced in the spiritual dimensions, to help present choices to us that will allow us to fulfill our desired and needed soul lessons.

PLANNING OUR LIVES

Why was it that after I made the statement that we script and plan our lives that my guides said, "Now we can tell you," and proceeded to give me a 24 hour life review of all the things I had done, said, and thought that were wrong or shameful? I think it's because if we didn't know that we planned our lives to learn certain lessons, and then were given a life review showing all of our negative thoughts and behavior, we would feel like helpless victims. We would feel overwhelmed, condemned to eternal shame and remorse.

Those who have near death experiences and those who die and undergo the life review are aware that there is a greater purpose or aware that they planned their lives and were meant to learn from them. That empowers you to know that what happened to you was supposed to happen and that it happened for a purpose, a reason, to learn from those experiences, however negative. They were meant for spiritual growth, and not a random heinous fate, or the punishment of a cruel God.

Shanna Spalding St. Clair's book states that we create our own journey. Neither can we take on responsibility or blame ourselves for someone else's life path.

Kelvin Cruickshank says everything that happens to us is meant to happen. There are no coincidences – we have chosen the hurt, pain, and experiences to foster our personal development, to graduate and grow as a soul into a more complete understanding. He describes it as earning our wings. We are meant to learn from the experience, recognize it for what it is, and then move forward. Since our thoughts, feelings, emotions, and intentions determine who we are, we wouldn't grow and learn from our own decisions if we didn't make them.

He adds that on a soul level we know our plan and realize the purpose of our life. We are able to change our attitudes, and meant to find the lesson, to gain strength and understanding, and make the negative positive.

As medium Austyn Wells says, we are not to accept the role of victim, but to learn from our mistakes to make better choices. We can ask for help in accomplishing our goals but ultimately must make our own decisions. It is what we make of our experiences that counts.

Shanna Spalding St. Clair's book comments, "Obstacles are to be met with positive solutions."

I have heard that we must live in the present, learn from the past, and work toward the future.

We carry the lessons from the past with us, it is said. Through those lessons we project and design a better future. But we must live in the present. It is there where we act, think, and make choices. Many mediums say that we can be shown past lives or incidents from our past that will shed light on our current situations and problems, and that, to an extent, the future can be known in that certain events are set in place by our plans, intentions, and current circumstances.

Some events are planned in this life as lessons we intended to learn. However, this is all tempered by our free will, with which we can change circumstances and future events. Some of these are part of a soul contract previously made and are not changeable, but many are lessons that can be learned in various ways. Therefore, most of our future lies in probabilities. Future events can be discerned by those who have that ability, but many of these can be altered, while some, according to soul contract, cannot. We can always change our reactions to events.

NEGATIVITY AND POSITIVITY

I am told that all good things, including soul growth, developing unselfish love, overcoming negativity, learning and growing, are not instantaneous. Such things take time and effort as well as discipline. They require a belief in ourselves, with faith and trust. It takes effort to acquire knowledge and experience.

My guide gave me a good analogy. He said we should never be ashamed when we get our hands dirty in life because that means we are learning lessons. If we never get our hands dirty, we aren't learning them. If we can never say we've done something wrong, then we aren't making progress.

When I see others stumble, I always say, "There but for the grace of God go I", because, as humans, we all share foibles and weaknesses, and, as such, share the capacity for error if we are in their circumstances.

Many mediums have communicated statements that we must work to trust in ourselves and in spirit. We must develop belief and understanding that positive attitudes allow us to grow, help ourselves and others. Knowledge must be acquired by both reading and experience. We not only learn by experiencing the outcome of our own choices, but also by observing the examples of others, and by vicariously reading or discussing options. Mediums have indicated that guides and those who love us in spirit will never let us fall or fail. Anytime we feel we failed or have fallen does not indicate that we truly have failed, but that we have learned a lesson which we can take with us to improve our future performance. All of these lessons, even the so-called failed ones, are a part of soul growth and therefore necessary and helpful. It is also stated that discipline accelerates our growth and helps us to improve in our practice of mediumship. It is stated that we are never alone, but always supported from the other side.

Kelvin Cruickshank writes, negative experiences can help us to grow stronger as well as to understand others. By growing spiritually, we become better people. Although the lessons we need to progress can cause anger and bitterness, these impede our progress and we must seek constructive solutions to advance and benefit from the lessons.

A constructive solution might be starting an organization to help other parents who have lost children to cancer if you have lost your own. A negative reaction would be suicide or submission to drug addiction. I have previously discussed a real-life situation I was told about by an acquaintance whose brother had suffered the loss of a limb in a motorcycle accident. My acquaintance's brother had gone on to poverty, drug addiction, and death, while another person with a similar injury had gone on to be the first one-legged skier to helicopter ski from the top of a high mountain. I like this example because it illustrates two very different reactions to a similar event, one positive and one negative, one constructive and the other destructive.

I've had to apply these principles in my own life. Sometimes troubles seem to inundate us. Recently I lost a beloved pet needlessly, and a month later two others were diagnosed with incurable illnesses. I've had difficulties with some ruthless coworkers on the job and, earlier in my life, some negative and exploitive personal relationships. I've experienced gender inequities and various forms of prejudice, not to mention the painful loss of loved ones. Knowing there is another life after this present one gives comfort, but doesn't insulate us from all the pain of negativity and loss.

I've asked myself, how can you be positive when negative things happen? I can't correct them or ignore them. I realized that we have to try to remain positive in spirit, as the worldly insults never go away while we are alive in the flesh. I recall the phrase in the Bible that in the world we will have trouble, but in spirit we will find peace. I try to keep this foremost in my mind and adjust my attitude when troubles beset me, knowing I have a better life awaiting me in spirit.

Sometimes a change of attitude is all we need to move forward in our lives. I no longer look at myself and think I know so little. I wish I could do more. But I look at others and think, "I'm so glad they can give that much help or how wonderful they can break ground, provide a path for us, show us the way and inspire us."

I'm happy when what I do is adequate to contribute, even if in a small way. God knows my heart and will make it possible for me to contribute in a way that is adequate to my progress and will help me to move forward and learn that I, too, may contribute more.

God knows what is right for me and will enable me with my effort and his wisdom, to achieve it. Sometimes when we don't achieve the entire magnitude of our plans and goals, it could be because we are not ready yet. Maybe there is something else we need to learn or experience before we are competent to accomplish our desired mission. I've heard the comment that when the teacher is ready the pupil will appear and vice versa. Sometimes, if we are not in a position to achieve what we want, maybe we are meant to take an alternate route. I am thankful for other people's gifts and thankful that mine will develop and grow appropriately.

ENDING NEGATIVE RELATIONSHIPS

Sometimes we have to receive help from spirit to move forward with our lives, to become more assertive and lose our fear, to assert our own power and destiny, and not be a captive to others' pressure, domination, or control. Sometimes we need to learn faith in ourselves and courage of conviction. This means owning our own power and taking charge of our future.

It does not mean selfishly trampling over the needs or desires of others. It does not mean refusing to compromise or learn. It does mean not allowing others to manipulate us or use us, deliberately harm us, dominate us, usurp our freedom, or control our destiny against our will. When we allow others to exploit us or control us to the negation of our own free will and choices, we do this out of fear. This means fear of the consequences if we protest or stand up against those who are controlling us. This means fear of what will happen if we assert our own individuality and free will or choice. In order to reject or refuse domination, we must overcome our own fear, step out, and act regardless of the consequences.

There are always people in line to tell us what to do with our lives. There is that old saying that too many cooks spoil the broth. Their advice comes from their own belief system, opinions, and desires, and may not coincide with what is "right" for us. To give an example, I had a cousin who was offered free tuition to veterinary school by his animal-loving grandmother, but he refused to accept it, knowing he wouldn't be happy as a veterinarian when he desired to be in law enforcement. We have to take our own journeys and fulfill our own objectives. Others can't live for us, and if we conform to their desires, we will never fulfill our own dreams or be happy, ourselves.

There is such a thing as good advice and being made aware of alternatives and options. That is not negative. It is wise to consider outcomes before we jump into a commitment. We may heed or reject that advice, but, either way, we are meant to learn from our mistakes if we make them so that we do not engage in a cycle of repetitive self-destructive behavior. A relative's mother told him as a child, "A hard head makes a soft rear-end," which in my experience is good advice. I've been there a few times.

Things that I have read through other mediums are that when that lesson is learned, when we have accomplished this, that the relationships which are domineering and negative will either change or fall away and be removed from our lives, as we no longer need them as a lesson to stand up for ourselves, be ourselves, and achieve our own destiny.

FEAR OF LOSS

One thing that must be addressed when we eliminate negative patterns in our lives is fear. Have you ever heard anyone say, "I just can't believe that anything this good could ever happen to me?" Years of negative treatment can undermine our self-esteem and make us feel doubtful and unworthy. We can all learn to make better choices that give us a better chance of finding happiness, but none of us earn it. It is a gift. But we also have to accept it.

We shouldn't let previous losses make us fearful that they will continue or recur. We have power, control to a certain degree, and choices of how we will react. We are not all powerless to the whims of an unfeeling fate, but have options and can affect our outcome to a certain extent.

We can't always have that perfect outcome we desire. Even though mediums often like to say that there are no coincidences and we are always right where we are supposed to be at any given time, there are such things as random accidents, and we also are subject to the free will and decisions of others. It is a complex, interwoven web or network.

We can't change chance or how others behave, but our free will can determine our direction. We can't control what others do or say, but we can control our reaction to them. We must first set our intentions, and then act in accordance with our desires. Of course, there are some circumstances beyond our control, but we don't have to acquiesce and become victims of fate, casualties of random coincidence.

We have to play with the hand we are dealt, but we must proceed with trust and faith, work at accomplishing our destiny, and direct our energy with positive efforts. Life is never easy, but we don't have to be automatons or puppets.

A friend told me that as long as you get up one more time then you've been knocked down, you haven't lost the fight.

Kelvin Cruickshank states that we must create our own life without fear, and that if we take wisdom and lessons with us, we will not fail.

I understand that one of our objectives on this earth is to overcome fear and negativity, to stand firm in our purpose and act in love.

I have heard other mediums make statements that only when we face fear and choose to overcome it will we really gain the strength we need to accomplish our hearts' desires. Doing that which we think we cannot do, such as living through a tragic loss of a child, husband, wife, parent, or loved one, we realize our inner reserves of strength and courage. We grow through such experiences and are able to give and help others also endeavoring to overcome grief, loss, and disappointment. We attempt to find something positive in the negative, to persevere as souls, and help others to persevere until we are reunited with those we love on the other side.

FREE WILL AND GUIDANCE

No one can learn for you, or take a test for you. We can ask for and receive inspiration or advice, but we have to stand or fall on our own.

Kelvin Cruickshank says that spirit can't live your life for you. They can only give you hints about the right direction. We must make the choices. We always have many options, doors, or roads, and it is up to us which one to take. We have an intuitive grasp of right and wrong, but must make our own decisions because they make us who we are.

Often, choices are not all "black or white", "right or wrong". There may be good and bad consequences to any decision you make. Not all choices are either all bad or all good. There are many options in between.

Once we have made a particular choice that leads to unhappiness we may not be able to erase the consequences or completely reverse its effects. We are entitled to happiness but must consider the effects of our behavior upon others and reach a compromise that is best for all concerned — ourselves and others — and avoid gratification of our own desires if fulfilling them is at the expense of severe destruction or harm to others. Conversely, we must not be prisoners to the domination of others, sacrificing our own fulfillment for the gratification of someone else's selfish demands. Once a "bad" decision has been made, sometimes negative consequences are inevitable, but solutions must be worked out with regard for the feelings of all involved, both others and ourselves, seeking resolution that, while imperfect, is in the best interest of all involved.

But seeking not to harm others, providing compassion and service, acting in honesty and love, and respecting ourselves and others permits for a great deal of individual freedom in goals, choices, and attainments. Among these choices we must find what is right for us.

HELP IN MOVING ON

I have been told that advice and help are always available to us if we ask. It doesn't mean that we're given the answers to the test, because then we would never learn the lesson. It does mean that advice, help and support are available to us if we ask and listen. Those who are our loved ones and guides in spirit are interested in our welfare and best interests and are there to help us and love us.

I reflect on some of the ways in which I overcame the pain of the past to the extent that I have been able to move on. There was a time when I was, for lack of a better word, paralyzed by the trauma of the past. No matter how much I thought about it, pondered it, evaluated it, and analyzed how I could have done things differently and achieved a better outcome, I couldn't get past it emotionally.

I felt as though I were stuck on a treadmill, and no amount of mental manipulation could get me off. I had to work through all of the issues, consider all of the alternatives, and figure out how I could have changed what I did, and what the outcome would have been with others if things had been different on my part.

I couldn't receive the help from messages being given me because I was in a state of emotional trauma. I needed extra help at a crucial moment and was given it. Somehow, I knew then, that I had progressed through enough emotional healing inside that I could receive the messages I needed. But I knew I couldn't completely heal without that love and assurance. I knew that one more clear assurance from spirit would kick start me over the obstacles in my mental embankment.

That was when I particularly asked for help from someone I loved on the other side, for support and assurance. My loved one, so patient with me, gave me that assurance, which at last enabled me to drop the baggage and heal from the past. By heal, I don't mean that I forgot the pain. I mean that now the pain no longer controls me or dictates my thoughts and actions. That pain no longer has power over me to stymie me, to prevent me from moving forward. The nightmare portion of the past is now over. I never have to relive it. I never have to go through it again.

Those who love us never give up on us. They stand by us even when we are weak and when we fail. It was that kind of help from my loved one, that generosity of spirit, that enabled me to overcome the impasse. I am very grateful to my loved one in spirit for that last nudge, that last act of love and kindness, which enabled me to do that pole vault over the last hurdle. Because of that I am no longer a prisoner to the past. That love and support gave me the power to slay the dragon. Pain can be reawakened when I think of the events. But because of that last statement and confirmation from my partner, I am free to move on into a better life with my loved one. I am no longer trapped.

Occasionally something I hear or see still triggers insecurity. All of those bad memories and feelings are right there waiting to be recalled. They don't go away. We can feel them as acutely as we did when we were living through them if we allow ourselves to do that. I have actually kept a journal of all the beautiful positive and loving things that have come though to me from my loved one in spirit circles. When I get that occasional twinge of fear I reread what he has said to me and remind myself that that was then and this is now, and I don't have to go through the loss and hurt again. It's in my mind and I have to make a choice to permit it to dominate me or to tell it I have power over it. Our thoughts can sometimes be our own worst enemy. When I need a little more emotional support, my loved one will give me a subtle reminder or a few words of assurance that are like a hug, and that helps me to put the past and the fears that it will recur back in their place.

ENDING NEGATIVE CYCLES

In reviewing my life, I recognized a pattern of accepting abuse and exploitation, which engendered trust and self-esteem issues. I had become bitter, and, like so many other people, wondered why me?

What changed me was love. I wanted to change me, to change my life, to become a better person, both for myself and for the person I love. That was when I received a humbling life review from spirit. I was presented with my own shortcomings and mistakes, as well as the fact that mistreatment from others had made me poisoned and bitter.

When I saw these incidents more clearly, I realized that some of the mistakes I made hurt me far more than the acts of others. When I recognized how much I needed forgiveness, too, if I could be forgiven, I knew I could forgive what others had done to me. At that moment I was able to forgive them. Forgiving myself was more difficult.

Not only did I make the effort to change my own life, but I was no longer willing to accept denigrating treatment from others. Only when we have the courage to look at our own lives and identify the part we play in perpetuating negative cycles, can we change them. I believe that love and lack of love were important lessons in my lifetime. I learned that I don't want to live in a world without love. When we fail to love we destroy one another.

But we must not let the wrong of others change us. If we allow someone else's mistreatment to poison us, we can become as bad as our persecutor. We must not let bitterness, anger, and resentment cause us to become like our tormentor. Remaining positive entails setting boundaries, not willingly allowing others to harm us, forgiving, acting in kindness, and looking inward to spirit for strength throughout the disappointments of life. Only when we choose to act in love can we maintain harmonious relationships and positive lives.

Kelvin Cruickshank encourages us to not keep repeating the same mistakes, but to connect with our Creator and remain true to our sense of right and wrong, to be positive despite the insults of life. He states, if there is abuse, we are meant to break the cycle.

ABUSE, HEALING, AND FORGIVENESS

Kelvin Cruickshank states that when there is abuse, we are meant to break the cycle. When someone has abused us, we are not to take on blame, as though we are unworthy or responsible for the negative treatment. Nor do we forget abuse, but we can forgive, and when we do, it sets us free.

He advises us to ask for help from spirit to understand it, and let it go. We can get trapped by the behavior of others if we are a victim or can't forgive ourselves if we are a perpetrator. Forgiveness is the key that permits us to move forward, to heal, and to release bitterness.

It is easier to forgive when we see our own errors, our own mistakes born out of ignorance. There is a plethora of adages in the literature about judgment. In the Bible, Jesus had said, "He who is without sin, let him cast the first stone." "Judge not lest ye be judged with the same judgment." Another aphorism is, "Those who live in glass houses should not throw stones."

I have a personal account. I had a relative who got involved in some negative circumstances. I once encouraged her to seek a different direction. I guess to a certain extent I judged her in my heart when she didn't. I was wrong. Although she now lives in the afterlife, she has come through to teach new mediums in training and has helped me by providing answers to some of my questions. We are friends, appreciating each other. I have learned a lot from her. She had a very difficult and traumatic youth and although I didn't make the same choices she did, I have made others just as bad but different. I think we all need to walk a mile in each other's shoes before we judge each other because none of us is perfect and we haven't experienced the same trauma another person has. If we wish to be forgiven, we must also forgive. The Bible also says, "Mercy triumphs over judgment."

If we carry no remembrance of the negative events of our lives, we would have no understanding to help us avoid those situations in the future. But to let fear paralyze our lives because of them is to allow them to continue to dominate us. Or to be unwilling to forgive, if we can, permits us to carry bitterness and resentment, burdens we shouldn't have to carry, that prevent our forward progression, as well as the progression of those who have harmed us.

Only in mutual forgiveness can we all free ourselves from the injuries of the past.

RELEASING THE FETTERS

Why are anger, resentment, bitterness, and guilt so bad?

Certainly, if we wrong others or are wronged by others, these are common reactions. We don't live in a perfect society or a perfect world, and eliminating these feelings entirely isn't possible.

But in a spiritual sense, they are destructive emotions because they tie us to a negative event and hold us back from moving forward. Instead of seeing better solutions and more positive experiences, they anchor us to unhappy feelings, not allowing us to move past hurts or mistakes and find happiness.

Allowing ourselves to forgive ourselves and others liberates us to grow and make our lives and decisions better. This isn't easy, but the outcome is well worth the effort.

Many times, when spirits fail to cross over after death, it is because of those residual emotions, anger over some insult or injustice, or fear of consequences for some bad deed they have done. Others can simply be tired to a place they loved or unwilling to leave a person they cherished. While remaining near the earth plane is permitted and not necessarily bad, being anchored there because of guilt, anger, or fear is restricting and spirits can build their own prison of sorts. Insight, new awareness, healing, encouragement, and guidance may help such spirits to move forward and acclimate themselves on the other side.

Others may have a positive reason to stay near the earth plane, to be guides or guardians to those they love.

DISCARDING EMOTIONAL BAGGAGE, MAKING BETTER CHOICES

As I indicated earlier, when I began getting messages from my spirit guide, I got a lot of good advice, but couldn't implement it without first working through problems from the past, including mistakes, regrets, and anger over mistreatment from others. Emotional baggage was holding me back.

In order to release it, I first had to understand why these things happened, what I could have done about them, and how different actions on my part would have altered the course of my life. Understanding what I could have done to produce a better outcome is part of learning the lesson.

Once the past, including the mistakes, regrets, and anger were dealt with mentally and emotionally, only then could I move forward.

My spirit guide gave me invaluable help and advice, emotional support and assurance that enabled me to let go of these balls and chains. Knowing what happened, why it happened, and what I could have done about it freed me.

All of these things are there, a record in my soul, but they no longer dominate or control me. I was meant to benefit by learning from them, not reliving them, or letting them make me fearful of the future.

When a negative pattern is exhibited in your life, it's easy to see why you would fear that it would happen again and again. This cycle is self-defeating and sabotages the future. I had to first realize the part I played in contributing to and permitting the negative pattern to develop before I could break the cycle by changing my outlook, thoughts, and behavior.

Changing our attitudes and behavior is a process that doesn't prevent negative things from happening to us, but changes the way in which we cope with them, enabling us to no longer be overpowered by them or victimized.

The best action is to heed warning signs and avoid jumping into situations without carefully assessing them, because you may be able to prevent the problem in the first place. Once you are committed or entangled physically, emotionally, financially, or legally in a negative situation, it may be much more difficult to extricate yourself from it, and you may face unpleasant consequences or impact the welfare of dependents. Repercussions can involve the choice between two bad alternatives.

Ignoring negative situations or constant conflict both cause tension and stress, making daily survival a burden. Constant strife and conflict is detrimental to the mind, soul, and body. Continuously ignoring mistreatment doesn't eliminate ill-effects or eliminate it. Living in a negative situation consumes a lot of mental energy and peace, but leaving may also be very difficult and pros and cons must be weighed.

One lesson to learn from such predicaments is strength - either to endure or leave. If you fail to set boundaries, you are not respecting yourself, and there may be nothing left of you for yourself or anyone else. Allowing yourself to be abused, degraded, or taken advantage of is a disservice to yourself and your own self-respect. Refusing exploitation helps to diffuse anger, decrease damage to your self-image, and prevent trust issues.

Being nice or kind can sometimes evolve into being a doormat or a target for others who are predatory, and refusing to permit that, learning to say no, is a self affirmation. Being helpful should not be equated with accepting mistreatment. Placing a spiritual bubble of protection around yourself can deflect some negativity, but only when you refuse to accept such treatment will you begin to eliminate it from your life and become a happier person.

No one can prevent or avoid all negative circumstances. We cannot foresee all harm or prevent others from exercising their free will. There is that often asked question of why bad things happen to good people. One answer is that it "rains on the just and the unjust". By virtue of living in a society that permits free will and a world of imperfection, sometimes we are at the mercy of other people and circumstances.

When I lost my beloved dog, a compassionate veterinarian who is also a friend, wrote me some words of sympathy that touched my heart. She said, "When you lose someone you love, you don't get over it, you just get through it." My guide came through at a spirit circle and gave me some good advice. He showed himself swimming and doing the breaststroke, and said, "Sometimes you just have to push through all the muck, and there is great reward when you do." I asked him whether he meant great reward for us on earth or on the other side, and he responded, "On earth." I take that to heart now when I am in a difficult or negative situation, knowing that I don't currently live in Heaven or in a vacuum, and some things that I can't fix I just have to plow through.

PURPOSE AND PROGRESS

When you're young it isn't that the deep questions of life aren't thought of or important, but, surrounded with friends and relatives, and excited by future prospects of love, career, ambitions, interests, and family, we are preoccupied with these. The major questions of life are sublimated to current endeavors and the end of our life seems like a distant dream. When we grow old, lose loved ones and relatives to death, endure physical disabilities and illness, and are past the early stages of family, love, and career, the end of our lives becomes an imminent reality and those eternal questions of the purpose of life and the afterlife become more important. We are more often looking backward, and less often forward. The busyness of our early life fades and the question of mortality, hidden behind the former endeavors, emerges.

I have been told that there are many levels of spiritual development in the afterlife, and that we come to earth for the purpose of learning, that we might progress and advance through those levels on the other side.

Statements that I have heard and read through other mediums indicate that there are advanced souls, some with greater wisdom, kindness, and love. I have also heard that there are negative spirits on the other side who were negative people when they were on the earth and did great harm to others. These souls may attempt to influence or harm living people who remain on the earth, and mediums have stated that when we open ourselves up to spirit communication, we need to protect ourselves and pray so that we are not harmed by those negative spirits. I have encountered numerous mediums who have had physical scratches or injuries, as well as pejorative comments or attempts to influence negative behavior in them from such spirits. I have personally heard negative comments and negative mental directives, as well as cursing and very negative comments which have come through the Spirit box.

Our purpose is to address our own weaknesses, improve our understanding, make more positive decisions, and help others to grow and do the same.

Kelvin Cruickshank states that inasmuch as we are in charge of our thoughts and emotions, we are in charge of who we are, the person we are. We must finish a situation and move forward, start over. As we are in charge of our thoughts, attitudes, and choices, we can control our dreams.

FWH Myers comments that we are put in the physical to develop the spiritual.

Charlotte Dresser communicates, that is the secret of it all — the upward climb.

A friend of mine who is a medium brought through my aunt, and conveyed the message that we are all on a stairway to Heaven.

Regarding concentrated thought, my guide channels, "As sunshine is the source of energy for the development of nature, of living things, spiritual nourishment is the energy source for our creative endeavors, and allows us to think about what we wish for and create ways of achieving it. We embrace our goal and perfect our attainment through our individual intense intentions."

In reference to using our energy, my guide states, "It is the productive use and direction of energy, cosmic energy, manipulated through our creative mind, transformed by and transforming our own life energy, the creative direction of force. It is like a course in applied physics, the utilization of energy."

My guide explains spirit interactions, "We interact for the mutual common good, for development to promote spiritual learning, to foster progress, to develop understanding, and to apply that beneficial awareness to our decisions, actions, and lives.

In this way, we transform ourselves and others for the common good.

Our lives are meant to be a positive energy source engaging in mutual inspiration, transmission of knowledge, and courses of action that benefit the whole. Our intelligence is meant to be directed, our efforts aligned with the principles of good, of helpfulness, of encouragement, of guidance. We learn, know, and help others to do the same.

We seek revelation, enlightenment, understanding, in the purposeful direction of our actions."

KARMA

Shanna Spalding St. Clair channels that we "transmute the outward manifestation of our existence in conformity to the need for karmic progression, going through successive continual incarnations until we no longer maintain form when we reunite with Source.

Karma results from our choices and deeds and its purpose is to overcome the negative and to choose the positive. Our path is our chosen set of circumstances and experiences in a given life that will allow us to learn a needed lesson, change or improve our understanding, choices, and behavior.

We incarnate for karmic interaction, designed to advance the mutual progression of the group of light beings with the goal being enlightened choice. Evil is meant to provide opportunities for obstacles to be met with positive solutions and all experience, even the tragic, is meant to direct us to positive thought and action.

We cannot force other souls to have spiritual fulfillment, but only facilitate their attaining it. Love is the most powerful energy and is capable of providing great change. We must understand love in all of its aspects to perfect our knowledge of our purpose."

Gretchen Vogel indicates we incarnate to learn better choices that lead to happiness and healing.

Kelvin Cruickshank states that, as we are made in the image of God, we have good deep down. The spiritual mandate we are to observe is to not cause harm to others and to maintain our own self-respect.

Regarding the cycle of karma, you cease to perpetuate it by changing the intention and deed and by forgiveness. That is how you break the chain. In other words, if someone has done you wrong, you create a perpetual cycle by returning harm for harm. If you have the strength and courage to step outside the cycle, to react with positive behavior instead of returning negative for negative, you break the cycle. You become a victor by choosing good. Your real enemy is negativity, more than the person who harmed you, and the only way to defeat that enemy is by not acting like the person who wronged you, defeating negativity by reacting with love rather than retribution. That does not mean inviting others to continue harming us or failing to protect ourselves from the perpetrator of wrong, nor does it mean we have to love the bad deed they did. It just means that we break the cycle of vengeance. That is true power over the greatest enemy – the desire to harm others. Are we all strong enough to do this? No. But I admire those who are. I recently watched a documentary about a man whose young child was raped and murdered. He had the opportunity to exact vengeance and kill the man who did the heinous crime, but fought his inner rage and chose not to do so. He said he thought about the example he would have been giving to his other living children if he had retaliated and killed the murderer, and that alone prevented him from doing it. That was a very emotionally charged program.

Past life regression is meant to help someone by exposing past life trauma in the hope that awareness of a past negative event will help us to overcome its influence on us in our present life. The theory is that you change the carrying forward of a physical ailment by healing the spiritual trauma, and it will cease to manifest in the physical. You can also surmount emotional fears tied to prior past life experiences by becoming aware of their origin and breaking their hold over you with fear.

The elimination of the karmic debt requires not only forgiveness, but willingness to perform an act of kindness toward the perpetrator rather than an act of retribution or vengeance. That is purportedly how the karmic cycle is broken.

TRANSPARENCY

My guide expresses, "The truth will be made clear. Nothing will be hidden from us. No one will be denied the truth or held in darkness. We are not left to misunderstand things or wonder about them.

When we have had a relationship on earth, we each know what the other has done and how they reacted. We may not know everything, but we do know everything that pertains to us, everything that affected us, whatever is important or vital to our knowledge for our growth and understanding.

No one will be left unaware or uninformed. The truth will be known by all and revealed in our life review. Some may want to conceal things, but they are unable to do so. No one can lie.

We and others could not learn lessons from our lives if the truth about what we each did and what really happened were withheld from us.

Those who contemplate remaining together are made aware of all aspects of the relationship, and no one is kept together under false pretenses. Free will could not prevail in our decisions if we were forced to make decisions without adequate knowledge.

No one will ever be able to say I was never told. I didn't know. There is no deceit in the afterlife. True character is revealed and there is transparency in spirit. We work at forgiveness, and then move on."

ANSWERS FROM THE AFTERLIFE

I have encountered quite a few deceptive, dishonest people in my lifetime. When that person is someone close to you whom you trusted it can be quite a shock and disappointment. There were other "respectable" people who were doing very illegal things, some of whom were caught and prosecuted, but most were not. Experiences such as these can erode faith and trust in others, and life at times can feel like a battle where innocence is bliss. I am reminded of a saying in the Bible that "He who seeketh wisdom seeketh sorrow," and, What is done in the dark will come to the light." More and more those observations feel applicable in my life. Most often the truth eventually comes out. It is refreshing that in the afterlife, true characters will be revealed and we will know one another as we really are.

Kelvin Cruickshank indicates secrets can create darkness. A spirit can remain angry if there are unresolved feelings and hurt. Love is about being truthful. Love is eternal. We should tell our loved ones the truth about our lives. Secrets bring negativity. We should have no unfinished business. We should be honest and tell others the truth up front. We should not entice them into a situation unknowingly or blind.

TRUST AND SERVICE

Kelvin Cruickshank states that we need patience, trust, and faith. We will be given what we need.

We are only given knowledge that we are capable of understanding and assimilating at our current stage of development.

When giving readings, I've noticed that it is the person who needs it most who gets the message. When you get up to give a message you have to forget ego, forget fear, and trust. The reason you should be giving a message is to help the spirit and the recipient, not for your own pride. I was giving messages for the right reason, but let fear of failure ambush me. It's scary when you're standing up in front of a group of people and what you say may be very crucial to someone who is grieving the loss of their loved one. Self doubt would creep in and I would think, "What if I say the wrong thing and hurt someone or look like an idiot?"

One day I realized that I would never move forward if I didn't make that leap of faith and trust. I thought, "Why am I here?" If I waste this time I'm given to do good by letting fear prevent me from giving messages, I'm throwing away this gift. That's when I decided to stand up and talk. It's always easier to sit and observe others take chances, but you'll always be a bench-warmer that way. It's not about me or my vanity. It's about Spirit, and I decided to serve Spirit. Now when I feel timid or insecure, I remind myself, it's not about me. I stand up and say what I hear, regardless of the consequences.

Answers from the Afterlife

No one — even the most experienced medium — is ever 100% accurate all the time. It's what's in your heart. I'm not the greatest, but I do what I can to the best of my ability. I'll go out on that limb. If you try your best and have an earnest heart, Spirit will let their love shine through you.

Charlotte Dresser channels, those who serve most are the greatest here.

"Claude's Book" states, our inner being is transparent. We cannot hide our true character or lie.

COMMITMENT

My guide indicates, "The real commitment is in the heart, not on paper. If you haven't made the commitment in the heart, you won't honor the one on paper.

In relationships, you can't make a commitment that is one way. The other person must make a commitment too, which includes both honoring that commitment and both providing effort to make it work. Both must work at the commitment together to make it viable.

I learned that commitment is in your heart and if you have it in your heart, it is a true one. Otherwise you have no real or lasting commitment.

Honoring something by force is a forced obligation, not a commitment. A legal contract is just that, and is temporary. The lasting commitment is spiritual, not physical.

You can't make a commitment unless the other person is in concert and then you must both honor it with your actions, words, and deeds.

A commitment is from love, not force, and love in itself is a commitment, an unwritten commitment.

What you speak with your heart comes out in your deeds, whether true or false, honorable or dishonorable."

PERSONAL AND HUMANITARIAN LOVE

I have been told that not all spirits love one another in an individual sense. Although I have been given an indication that there is an agapeic or altruistic, unconditional love in the afterlife, the type of love that God has for us, I have been told that spirits work to develop that type of love in the afterlife, and that this is a humanitarian type of love in which they choose to help one another and assist each other in their forward progress. In other words, they aid each other on their journeys. Some spirits who were very negative and harmful with others in their lifetime may not have that type of love and remain negative for a longer or shorter period of time in the afterlife, until they learn lessons and are able to discard their negativity.

There is also an individual love that spirits have for those with whom they have formed bonds, those with whom they are most compatible. Comments from mediums which back up this type of idea include the statement that if there is no love, there is no connection. Also suggesting this concept is the comment that we go over to those we love. In addition, there are comments that the bond between those who love one another in spirit or in the flesh is never broken. All of these comments imply that there are some who do not love one another personally.

Backing this up in an individual sense is the observation that those who come through to us in spirit are our loved ones, friends, and family. Strangers can occasionally come to help but this is not nearly as common. Also, when we are told that we are being watched over and protected and loved, this is often by our former loved ones who have crossed over, as well as guides and guardian spirits or angels. This never appears to be random, and it is seldom indicated that we are watched over by strangers, or people that we have had negative relationships with in the past.

When spirits come through, it is usually to those left behind in the physical with whom they have had very strong bonds of love. It is usually when there were very deep ties of love that a spirit comes through stating that they will always be with their loved one in the physical, and the spirit may stay with them as a guide or guardian.

I have been told that earthly relationships in which there has been great love, happy relationships, can be continued in the afterlife, and such relationships predispose those who had them to continued close ties in the afterlife. Relationships which had been very negative or harmful and unhappy on the earth usually are accompanied by forgiveness, discussion, assessment, mutual understanding of what each soul learned from the other, making peace, and then most often separating or going their own ways. This does not mean that those who had those feelings cannot choose to help one another or come together for a purpose, such as a reading for a child, but I have been told that most often people who had abrasive, unhappy, or harmful relationships in life usually do not remain together on the other side, or do not see one another often, their separate and different outlooks causing them to go in different directions without malice.

As such, when there have been disruptive and tension-filled relationships on earth, souls do not necessarily maintain a close connection in the afterlife or remain together, but they do not perpetuate the harm and come to terms with one another, learning from their experiences and moving forward, leaving malice and pain behind, each on his own journey.

Comments delivered through mediums in readings that back up this concept include ones given by husbands and wives separated by death that they had nothing but happy memories and admiration for one another while they were alive. They had a great love and respect for one another while living, which continues beyond death. Some mediums indicate that spirits who are together present themselves as holding hands, or with their arms around one another, while those who have chosen to separate, stand apart. One medium told me that if that small spark of true love was present between people they could choose to stay together. When it wasn't there, they most often go their separate ways.

Not all souls love all other souls in an individual or personal sense. There is individual love, there are individual bonds, and some souls love one another much more intensely than they do others.

Other comments that support the idea that there are deeper bonds of love between some souls have come through mediums in which former husbands and wives state that they are together and are very happy, that when one passed earlier the other missed their partner so much who had gone ahead all those years. One member of a couple who had been separated by death stated that he still missed and wanted the other. Sometimes the husband who has passed states that he is waiting for his wife. One partner made the comment that he loved his wife as soon as he saw her and continues to love her now as much as he ever did. Another talked about how much he loved his wife and how much he missed their life together. Souls who've had happy relationships and desire to do so can remain close and wait for one another. When they choose to reunite, which must be a mutual decision, that spark of true love grows and deepens in the afterlife.

These comments indicate that we do have individual, personal loves and attachments as we did on earth, some that are much stronger than others, and that they continue in spirit. The love we had here on earth does not dissipate with the loss of the physical body.

My guide states, "We love all souls, but not equally. We do have some souls that we are closer to based on our own individual characteristics. We gravitate to those with whom we have a greater affinity. We are closer to some souls based upon past relationships, affinity, thoughts, personality, individual characteristics, and qualities. We are not equally compatible nor do we spend equivalent amounts of time with all souls. Some we love deeply, others less, and some we spend little time with. We don't see much of them. All souls do maintain a regard or respect for one another. We can have a deeper love based upon our experiences or qualities. We do all love each other in a humanitarian sense, but in a personal sense, not in the same way or degree."

I have heard of and known people who have an intense immediate draw to someone in their life with whom they've had very little interaction. Other mediums have indicated that these are soul connections that we have with that person, reflections of prior experiences with them either in other lives or in the afterlife.

My guide continues, "How would I describe the altruistic love of the afterlife? It is the expression of good will, loving kindness, benevolence, and altruism toward all souls. It consists of a concern for their well being, well-wishes, and a desire for the happiness of others. We provide help and learning experiences for one another, not vindictiveness or retribution, but rather kindness, forgiveness, and munificence."

My guide showed me an earthly charity such as the March of Dimes or St. Jude's Children's Hospital to illustrate the humanitarian love spirits have for one another on the other side. It is a cooperative effort to assist one another to overcome obstacles on their paths of self- development. It is an unselfish, charitable concern for their welfare, performed as service, not expecting compensation in return.

Kelvin Cruickshank comments that for him, if two souls come through close to one another, this indicates that they are completely compatible, totally in love, and happy to be back together. If they come through far apart, either one passed earlier than the other, or they are separated.

Toni Winninger, channeling a soul, indicates that marriages with former husbands and wives from one lifetime are a very insignificant thing in the scheme of eternity.

Raymond, communicating to Sir Oliver Lodge, comments that those in antipathy part ways and those in affinity remain together. Like attracts like.

English medium Robert Brown states that if that small spark of true love was there, they may choose to remain together, and, if so, that love continues to grow on the other side. Otherwise they separate.

My guide sums it up, "We can love someone, an individual soul, that we have a strong or deep attachment to because of who they are, because of an affinity, because of their personality, and we want to be with them.

We can have a love for all souls based on caring, wanting their welfare and progression, manifested in the way we help one another."

LASTING LOVE

I have also been told that the bond of true love never dies.

Mediums have brought through statements from spirits that the bond on earth and the one in spirit are built out of love. That bond is never destroyed if two spirits love one another. It remains throughout eternity.

Shanna Spalding St. Clair channels, "You are never separated from those you love. There is always a connection from soul to soul, whether in spirit or in body, for those who care for one another. There is no separation in spirit. There is never a loss of connection between two souls that truly love each other."

This statement, in itself, implies that there are souls who do not love one another in a personal sense, who do not have an individual bond of love.

Charlotte Dresser channels that those linked by the strong bond of love, affection, and sympathy have a psychic connection in proportion to those ties.

"*Claude's Book*" indicates there is always a link between the spirits of people who truly love each other, and, sometimes, in seeking the spirits of those they loved and lost, many have found their own souls. The love bond is eternal.

I have been told that although some spirits move forward in the afterlife when they have parted with their earthly partner or loved one, that others choose to remain with the loved one who is still alive, can become a guardian angel or protector, a guide or helper to that person, and can even remain with them always throughout their lifetime until that person crosses over and joins them.

Comments made through mediums that support this idea include those in which a husband has said that he watches over his wife at night while she's sleeping. Several spirit husbands have indicated that they would come and lie beside their wife in bed at night or stand at the foot of the bed. They can remain with their loved one to guide, protect, inspire, support, encourage, and watch over them. Sometimes, quite frequently, in fact, the loved one on earth is aware of or feels their presence.

I along with several other friends of mine have personally heard some mediums say that we must not remain attached to those we love who have passed because it prevents them from moving forward in the afterlife. Then I have heard other mediums say that a spirit partner chooses to stay close to their loved one on earth and be their guardian, waiting until they arrive and join them. I do not regard the other side as some reality show race to the pearly gates with this season's winner putting their blog on the ethereal internet, 10 best ways to beat your competition to Nirvana. The best answer I have heard is that we have eternity to grow and progress on the other side, so if a spirit chooses to remain close to their loved one in the physical and wait for them, they lose nothing, as we are all eternal. My loved one described the wait for one another as no more than an afternoon in the scheme of eternity. I love the way he put it and now have the courage to believe him rather than some of the mediums I used to think were so wise because they had more experience than myself. Your truth is the one between you and your loved one, not the dogma of some other medium, myself included.

UNIONS

Do all souls who were together on earth remain together on the other side?

My guide indicates, "We all decide whether we want to remain together. No one has to be together. No one stays together if they don't want to. We all have our own choices. It depends on how they feel about each other in the relationship. If they did love each other, they can choose to stay together. If they didn't, they leave. If you don't love someone, you just leave and go on your way. That's it. Each goes his own way and does his own thing.

No one is forced to stay with anyone."

The spirit group, Silver, channels, some souls have been together for eons and eons.

Kelvin Cruickshank indicates there can be an ultimate love with the souls madly in love with one another, an amalgamation.

Medium L channels, there definitely are pairings of spirits on the other side. They do refer to themselves as pairs, mates, couples, and unions. This is true on the third and fourth levels.

The outside superficialities of our earth lives are no longer important. The deep bond of true love and commitment is. Those who have a true bond of love remain together. That bond is never broken. If we were unhappy or incompatible with someone in our lifetime, we separate, or see very little of each other in the afterlife.

There is a spiritual commitment that can be made by two loving souls in the Akashic records, and it is a powerful thing. In regards to passionate intimacy, she writes, we serve a good God. If we need something, it will be provided for us.

Betty Bethards writes, there are unions on the other side if souls prefer. Marriages are not necessary but possible if people want. Husbands and wives can stay together. Some do. Some don't. There is no force. If there were multiple partners, you usually stay with the one you truly love. Growth and interests must be compatible.

Charlotte Dresser channels, companionships on the other side are higher and finer and more enduring than worldly ties. Companionship is dependent on congeniality. Families do not always stay together. Each goes the way he prefers. There is not as much importance to family ties. We are united more by congeniality. We are related by the thoughts we think, the ideas we cherish. The loves you develop are nearer and dearer than the ties of blood.

Finding a previously married couple no longer together, a soul channels, each goes to his own place where his congeniality is expressed. Many husbands and wives are not together. Some are. Blood ties are not as important as soul ties. Affinity pulls together. Not many are married in spirit, and it is only in spirit that the tie continues on this side. Comparatively few keep that tie here. Most are happier to go their own way.

Others such as Barry Eaton and a spirit channeling through Leslie Flint expressed surprise that some couples were no longer together.

Charlotte Dresser continues, we know our soul companions. Spirit meets its own. Your electromagnetic or vibrational signature calls persons of a similar attraction. We are attracted by the same thoughts, plans, desires, and tastes. We can come together with a soulmate and at last form a perfect union of wisdom and love.

Nora Spurgin discusses Emmanuel Swedenborg's comments on unions, stating that true loving marriages are perhaps God's greatest gift, in which the love of God is expressed between spouses and such marriages may be for eternity.

Gretchen Vogel comments that many couples stay together and many don't. We can stay together with those we love on earth but it must be mutual. Love is the key. People may have plenty of deceased relatives, but if there was no love between them in life, there may be no abiding attachment in the afterlife either. Couples and pets can stay together. We can also stay near a loved one as a guide or guardian.

John Scott conjectures that some unions are better than the best on earth and are probably eternal. We will not search without rest for completion. Unions made in the afterlife prove as happy as the best on earth, souls growing together, each helping the other in spiritual advancement to further heights.

Barry Eaton states that souls join through choice and it depends upon their soul relationship and level of development.

MERGING AND SEX

Shanna Spalding St. Clair channels, "If you ask whether there is the physical or emotional sensation of love, the experience of passionate love, when one is in spirit, whatever awareness is necessary for the progression of the soul in spirit will be made available to that soul."

Charlotte Dresser channels, you can choose to have the sense of touch. We can have intimate companionship. All the joys you have there will only be intensified. There is a spiritualized form of affection which is higher and finer than its material counterpart.

Craig Hamilton-Parker indicates, as the physical drives are absent, sex is no longer a priority. However, for those who have a psychological or emotional need, the sex act can be simulated or performed. People can choose to maintain form resembling the human body if they desire.

Merging souls blend thoughts, ideas, emotions, and feelings, achieving a temporary union that is more intimate than the sexual union in the physical body.

Betty Bethards indicates you can merge, but you can have sex organs if you want. This is optional. You can also have merging with sexual or nonsexual intent.

Medium L states, we can have a mutually shared union. In the afterlife we are able to create the illusion of having sex as we would have had it on earth, and it will feel real to us. Merging is a blending of two beings into one, so close we can't even conceive of it. It feels like emotional rapture or bliss. A sexual act can be part of what it is if so chosen.

FWH Myers states that we can re-create sexual experience on the plane of illusion.

Barry Eaton says on the other side sex can be expressed by merging and you can have sexual or nonsexual merging. This can be between partners and soulmates or others.

Jasper Swain's son channels, two souls merge in true spiritual union.

TWIN FLAMES

I have been told independently by several mediums that I have a twin flame who has passed. My loved one in spirit had communicated to me prior to those readings, "Wait until you see who I am", and "We are meant to be together."

Shanna Spalding St. Clair's channeled book describes twin flames as the closest of soulmates, that they watch over and ensure each other's continuing progression, and only incarnate together for a special purpose to prod one another to move forward.

Her book also indicates that after their reincarnated cycles on earth terminate, twin flames are united. I asked her personally if she takes that to mean that they are together or if they merge into a single soul. She indicated that she felt it meant they are merged into a single soul.

Cynthia Sandys also mentions twin flames in her book and Barry Eaton writes that twin souls exist and eventually merge.

LEVELS

Each to his own – seeking our own level

It is said that we are our own judge and jury, and based upon our life, go to the level where we belong. Frederick Sculthorpe comments that God's laws are absolutely fair. Who am I to complain when one's own self is both judge and jury?

The medium, E, says we will be with a group of like-minded kindred souls.

Matthew Smith, Arthur Findlay college tutor, channels a spirit, Albert, who says, we go over to those we love.

Charlotte Dresser channels, each goes to his own place. That is where his congeniality is expressed - to those of his own thought and purpose. We gravitate to our level of development with kindred souls. You will find those you really love. Tastes, outlooks, preferences, and desires determine our affinity. The law of attraction prevails. Your magnetic current draws those of similar attraction.

Anthony Borgia's book declares we gravitate to those of our own kind.

"Claude's Book" remarks, we gravitate to the level of development appropriate to us, and reside with kindred souls.

RECALLING PAST EXPERIENCE

Kelvin Cruickshank remarks, when we die and cross over, the soul retains itself. We are set free from the burdens of our earthbound experiences.

Shanna Spalding St. Clair channels, "One characteristic of the light body is that it will retain complete memory of its cumulative experiences."

Kelvin Cruikshank states, after death the soul can relive its past experiences with all the emotions.

FINDING MY OWN TRUTH

None of us living on the earth knows the truth in an objective sense. None of us can prove purpose, meaning, or values. Only the concrete, objective, material world can be measured or proven. What if anything lies ahead after death can be evaluated personally, but never subject to absolute proof or measured validation. Many of the most important aspects of life are a matter of belief or inner faith and conviction.

People have a myriad of beliefs, philosophical, religious, and spiritual. All of us must reach our own conclusions and face our own destiny or master. No one lives forever in the physical body, so whatever lies ahead, we all face it for better or worse. Some believe nothing lies beyond, and others have personal religious expectations and belief systems.

If none of the religions, none of the philosophers agree on everything, why mediums? They are humans too. And why spirits? If another life exists, as I believe it does, does that mean souls who survive are instantly omniscient and enlightened, with all truth and knowledge?

As on earth, souls can only express what they know, their own personal experience. The understanding of the afterlife that I have been given, is that it is vaster by far and more encompassing than our small earth world could ever be — infinite, eternal, and boundless.

What we can and do choose to experience as souls is as different as we are. We, in essence, find our own heaven — the one that appeals to and is appropriate to us. Each will find his own, create his or her own reality, as, to a degree, we do on earth, only with expanded or practically limitless choices.

I think that is why there are such varying descriptions of the afterlife. If you were to take someone from a remote jungle and another from a vast metropolis, their descriptions of life on earth would be extremely different — both correct, but representing alternatives.

I've often wondered why we don't get more descriptions of the afterlife from spirits. It is so difficult to come through, takes so much energy, and details are difficult to convey, that I imagine souls don't try unless they have a very good reason. I also imagine that, as we don't have a reference point, some of the very different aspects or features of the afterlife are difficult to put into words. There may not be an exact analogy.

Also, if we were meant to know all about the afterlife, we would not learn our lessons on earth. Part of the driving impetus for us to change is due to the negativity we encounter here, and knowing all about the afterlife and our purpose for being here may not serve our highest good or greatest interest.

I believe that those who are meant to find out will, and will seek out answers. Mediums say that all answers are within us, and that we can access them through meditation. Anything that provides greater awareness, enlightenment, or comfort is beneficial.

I have found answers that have provided comfort and peace for my soul. This was accomplished over a period of years and didn't come easily. Partly, that's because I had to gain the confidence to trust what I was hearing, to try to avoid incorporating my own opinions or beliefs into the message, and to overcome the sequela of my personal issues from the past.

I am now able to channel material more effectively and to have confidence in the answers.

DIFFERENT REALITIES

I used to be puzzled and disturbed when answers I got from the spirit world didn't match those I heard from other mediums. I don't mean answers or information regarding my deceased loved ones or facts about their lives.

I mean answers to questions I had about what life on the other side is like. Some people don't care, some are curious, and some find this very important, as I do, perhaps because they want to know what their relationship will be like with their loved ones, or perhaps because they missed something that was extremely important to them on earth.

So whenever there were significant discrepancies in those answers I immediately thought, he or she is a professional medium, with many years of seasoned experience. I'm a relative newcomer compared to them and I work in a different professional capacity. I must be wrong and they must be right.

I suffered through quite a trial before I came to some other conclusions. I realized that on the other side there are many different opinions and values among spirits, as there are among people on earth. There is no complete uniformity or unanimity there either.

Are there some values that apply to all? I am told the principles of love, not intentionally harming others, the golden rule of doing to others as you would have them do unto you, and the assets of kindness, charity, mercy, forgiveness, unselfishness, service, and love are true spiritual values.

This does not mean that everyone practices them to the same degree, but that they are universal values of our Creator.

Why else might there not be agreement in other capacities on the other side? Because we remain individuals with individual choices and freedom. There are many desires, goals, and preferences not written in stone that are options available to each individual, and all different. The afterlife is vast and permits many varying choices.

Many things are not absolute and are open to choice. Another factor that can be considered is the varying levels of spiritual development. There are levels of understanding and truth that are only available to those who are capable or ready to understand them based upon their level of spiritual development. I have heard that we are only given knowledge or awareness that we are ready to receive, that we are capable of understanding and incorporating. Mediums, apart from their abilities as a medium, have different levels of spiritual development or advancement as do other souls.

I learned that what may be true in my case, my reality, is to a large extent created by me and those who are my closest companions, and may be very different from the circumstances of other mediums or souls in the afterlife.

That is why I no longer become worried, upset, or frustrated when another medium says something about the afterlife that is very different from what I heard.

PRUDENCE ANN SMITH MD

I realize that there are many different scenarios available, many choices, and that within general confines we make our own truth based upon our own values.

I now have the confidence and conviction to trust what I've heard, trust spirit, and trust myself and the message I have been given. In fact, I have reversed to the degree that I trust my own truth is what I will experience rather than the truth that belongs to some other medium.

This has given me peace, hope, and fulfillment. I rest a much happier person in the faith that what awaits me will be the beautiful reality my loved one and I are co-creating, the fulfillment of the desires of my heart and my dearest dreams.

YOUR OWN JOURNEY- CHOICES IN THE AFTERLIFE

There are many frequencies and vibrations of love in the afterlife. Vibrations in the afterlife range from negative on the lower levels to divine in the highest levels.

One medium may have chosen to set her level of work to the vibration of divine love. She has tuned into that frequency only, and has tuned out other frequencies. It is like a radio station. She cannot hear or see the other vibrations of love.

Our ordinary range of hearing in the physical does not permit us to hear sounds that the dog's range can hear. We are deaf to sounds that they can hear.

As she is tuned into a particular frequency of divine love, she is blind to other frequencies and does not perceive them. That does not mean that those frequencies do not exist. It just means that she does not apprehend them.

That is why some say that individual or personal love is irrelevant or abolished. They are only looking at, attuning to, or aware of a very specific frequency in the spectrum of love.

They are not sensitive to the infinite possibilities and choices of the afterlife. The afterlife permits many ideals, choices, and options. These are dependent upon the individual desires and personalities of the souls. As is true on earth, we do not become robots, and not one way fits all.

Not only are there many different levels, but an infinite variety of choices and options available to and appropriate for each soul. As not one lifestyle, goal, or way of thinking would make every soul on earth happy, not one lifestyle, choice, or way of living, would make every soul in the afterlife happy, nor be appropriate for every soul. Allowing for individual differences and levels of development, each soul must choose their own direction, goal, and personal happiness. This is done in conjunction with souls who have a similar manner of thinking and similar personality characteristics and desires.

The afterlife is not generic or regimented. It is individually and mentally-based and reflects for each individual choices and options appropriate to them, for their growth, happiness, and fulfillment as souls. Love would not force souls into a way of life that would lead to unhappiness for them, but would permit them options to develop their own personal identity and joy with the restriction that they are not to harm or hurt others.

All will come into the happiness and truth that is appropriate to, designed for, and best suited for themselves, acknowledging and respecting individual choices, integrity, and differences.

Some are only aware of "their truth". They are only looking at a specific spectrum of the afterlife. That is not comprehensive. There are other writers who have written more comprehensively about the structure and nature of the afterlife. Others give only a specific description limited to a segment or portion of the afterlife, not its breadth and entirety. Mediums can connect with other energies of a similar perspective or interpret information based upon their own opinions.

I was given the words "selective orientation." It is not that those mediums writing about the afterlife are either right or wrong. It is that each is coming from a different perspective rather than categorizing a comprehensive view or overview of the afterlife. Each is explaining or depicting a portion with which they are familiar rather than attempting to give a total or encompassing view.

Not all journeys are ours. We each have our own unique journey. As all are different on earth, all are different on the other side with individual goals, perspectives, relationships, intentions, and priorities.

Not one thing fits all. We maintain our own individual perspectives and values.

When you hear another medium's comments about the afterlife, that often reflects or incorporates their own personal experience and impressions. No one has the whole truth, because the truth is different for each of us depending upon our viewpoint.

Our viewpoints are different as on earth. Do not feel that you have to conform to someone else's journey or that their journey is meant for you. You are meant to find and pursue your own journey. Each of us has a unique journey.

Is there a common denominator or absolute or universal truth, too?

Only not to harm others and to love. That is our only mandate.

We have our own personal plan and spiritual purpose. We have our own personal reality and objectives. We embrace and live within our own desire and framework. We have our own dreams and fulfillment.

If we were forced to assume the desires of others, we would not be happy. Our destiny and outcome are ours. Do not feel compelled to assume the destiny and journey of others.

Craig Hamilton-Parker indicates that what we experience in the afterlife depends to an extent on what we are like, what we seek, and what we are eligible for based upon our level of development. It can be similar to our earthly experience or vastly different. We will find those we really love.

CONFLICTING VIEWPOINTS

I have a friend who doesn't believe in demons. Other mediums describe negative or malicious spirits, demons, and some have had bad experiences with negative, harmful spirits. It is obvious that experiences and beliefs are different.

Some mediums say that you shouldn't attempt to hold onto those you have lost as you are inhibiting their forward progress, while other mediums say that some of the souls of your loved ones state that they are with you always. Is one medium right and another wrong? I think that each has a different set of experiences as well as a different set of viewpoints.

As there are many different relationships on earth, I believe many different relationships persist in the spirit world. Perhaps some spirits, depending upon their own nature and the relationship they had with their loved one, may be closer and wish to remain with them always, perhaps as a guide or guardian, while others may not have had as close a relationship, and wish to move on. That is true both on the earth plane and on the other side.

Are all earthly relationships equally close or devoted? Some marriages are deeply connected, and others apathetic or worse. Why should all be uniform, equal or identical on the other side?

It is always the ones we love who wait for us, watch over us, or take us to the other side. It is almost always loved ones who come through to us in spirit circles or dreams. Some spirits even describe closer connections and deeper love with some left on earth, becoming guides or guardians, referring to themselves as soulmates or as intensely close. Some spirits say their soul will always be with a loved one remaining on earth. Some live with a loved one and wait for them to cross.

All of these scenarios are possible and not one is right for all. It depends on the spirits involved, what they are like, what their relationships were and what they want. To say that only one specific option is available would be inappropriate.

As on earth, we make our own truth. Only the souls involved can determine the nature of the relationship. Some souls want their loved ones to move on with someone else, while others are waiting for their loved one to cross over. Someone else's way isn't necessarily your way. Someone else's journey is not your journey.

Many mediums describe some souls as remaining together and others as separating. They can show themselves as separate or holding hands or with arms around one another. Some souls describe themselves as together and happy together. It is up to the souls and the decision must be mutual.

CREATING YOUR WORLD

FWH Myers indicates, when we are in earthly form we only see a part of the picture. There lies the unreality of the material world. In this invisible world, there is infinite variety of conditions. The dead can only describe what they've experienced.

Shanna Spalding St. Clair channels, in spirit, one creates one's own reality.

Gretchen Vogel states, the afterlife is a self-directed mental and spiritual reality.

The medium L states, there are multiple realities. It depends on where you are. Your beliefs determine your reality. Other times there is a shared common reality.

Nora Spurgin states, all that is good in the physical world, whether it be food, drink, human affections or sexual intercourse, can be experienced in the spiritual world.

John Scott states, they can do what they like. They try to satisfy their desires and surprised, believe they are enjoying the real thing they remember. They repeat past experiences with their new increased powers and faculties.

Gretchen Vogel indicates, spirits can create a temporary reality with their belief system and continue earthly experiences on the plane of illusion. Spirits live on a plane of conceptual reality. We project our thoughts to create the reality we inhabit. It will seem as real to spirit as the physical world is to you. In spirit, one creates one's own reality. The thought forms we construct and inhabit are real to us. The dead shape their own reality. They can also have a common shared consensus reality. Gretchen Vogel states, everything we can imagine after death is possible to experience to some extent if only within our own mental reality.

Our experience is individual. It can be similar to the earthly experience or vastly different. It is originator dependent. We shape our surroundings to our vision. Our external reality is formed by concentrated thought.

The spirit group Silver says that what you manifest through your thoughts is always available to you.

Raymond states, spirits can come over with earthly desires. They may partake of earthly desires until weaned.

Gretchen Vogel says, we can relive our strongest desires that were unfulfilled by creating an experience and adapting the memory world to our desire.

The medium L channels, psychological desires can be retained and fulfilled by creating an experience that will feel real to the participant. Certain desires important to an individual may persist for a longer or shorter period of time, especially if they were particularly important to that person, or if they represented a deep psychological need, or were deeply desired but not fulfilled on the earth plane. These desires, if not harmful to others, can be fulfilled, even if by creating an illusory experience which will seem real to the participant.

"*Claude's Book*" states, all of the activities of their previous life can be reenacted if such is their will. These activities will seem real to them. They can gratify sexual desire, created by memories and imagination. They can live within the fantasy created by their strongest desires on earth.

A PLACE OF UNCONDITIONAL LOVE

I have been told that the afterlife realm of God is a place of unconditional love of God for spirits. There is none of the negativity in the afterlife that we experience on earth. Craig Hamilton Parker describes the afterlife as having laws that are more protective. Souls are protected, safe, and there is healing for those who have been injured and harmed in their earth lives. Souls learn to forgive one another and there is no judgment for the lessons that we learned. We judge ourselves by our words, deeds, thoughts, and actions in our lifetime and go to a level that is consistent with our prior behavior and development.

I have read and heard through a number of mediums that the afterlife is a place of divine, unconditional love where souls cannot hurt one another as they do on earth. Some souls describe the afterlife as a perfected earth life, without the negativity and drawbacks. It has also been said that souls forgive one another, and make peace. It has been said that no one judges anyone else's lesson or learning experience and that souls are helpful toward one another. An idyllic, beneficent, loving atmosphere prevails.

IDEOLOGIES

I have been told that certain ideologies on earth, certain religious tenets, certain cultural beliefs, are man-made, and pertain to the earth, but not the afterlife. Some mores, folkways, rituals, and religious restrictions or dogmas are not from God, but from man and will not persist in the afterlife.

Other mediums have indicated that such ideologies, or man-made belief systems, do not survive the passage to the next world. I personally have had several dear friends who were very religious in a particular denomination, and had very set beliefs, communicate to me through a medium that they were surprised about some things when they went to the other side and not about others. They indicated that some of their ideas, particularly in regard to religion, changed completely. The other side seems to entail an opening up to a deeper truth that unites rather than divides all mankind. Prejudices and exclusionary religious dogmas seem to disappear. I have heard that our particular religion doesn't matter. The choice of whether to hurt or to do good in the world is what really counts. We are all going to the same afterlife, but may be separated there according to our level of development, intentions, goals, and desires.

SOUL GROUPS

Soul groups are congregations of souls that reincarnate together to teach each other lessons.

Shanna Spalding St. Clair channels, "Soulmates are karmic task mates. We assist each other's forward movement."

Gretchen Vogel channels, we dance with each other.

Jeffrey Marks channels a spirit who says, we service each other on our journeys.

A group reincarnates in various relationships with the incarnation necessitating the advancement of all souls involved.

Individual members of a soul group may be closer or more distant in relationship, some very close, and others inharmonious, as in any family.

REINCARNATION

I have been told that we reincarnate, and that most of us have had many past lives. I've been told that I have had past lives, but I do not recall any of these.

Many mediums have brought through statements that we have multiple past lives, often with other souls with whom we have reincarnated in this life, as well as with others that have not reincarnated with us this time. They state that we choose to come back to earth to gain more knowledge, and to verify that we have learned from our past lessons. It is stated that the earthly learning experience is compressed, and allows us to learn much more quickly in the atmosphere of negativity than in the positive atmosphere of the afterlife. It has also been said that when we return to the afterlife, we are healed of our hurts and forgive one another, eventually retaining only the lessons and the love from any given incarnation.

In regard to memories of past incarnations, I have a friend who has experienced déjà vu. He describes having visited several buildings in New York City where he had an uncanny knowledge of where certain structural features were located without having ever visited that building before in this lifetime. Another friend describes her grandson as having an intense desire at the age of nine to visit an Egyptian museum in Cairo, and a strong interest in hieroglyphics. She said several mediums have independently told her that her grandson has experienced another life in ancient Egypt.

There is an old reference to a phrase, "From the mouths of babes...." I have learned a great deal from the reports of children who have memories of prior incarnations. These are significant because children, I believe, are less likely to fabricate than adults, and more spontaneous because they have not yet been conditioned to think within accepted guidelines or adhere to adult belief systems. Some of the information that they could not have logically obtained can be verified by search of historical records. As such, some of these frank and unbiased comments can be enormously enlightening for those of us who do not consciously retain afterlife or past life recollections.

Although I have no specific memories of any prior life, I have numerous times when writing spelled words without thinking with a spelling that I later learned was the preferred spelling from the English Renaissance, and not the contemporary American spelling, which looked "wrong" to me. I also had a deep interest in British Renaissance poetry from my teens, when I was enamored with a poem about eternity by Herbert Vaughn. I have always naturally written poetry in typical English meter and rhyme matching that from the English Renaissance period.

Was I there? I don't know. I can only say that I have certain natural abilities and proclivities that I was born with. Other children have demonstrated specific memories and provide details of another life in another time that have been researched and have proven accurate.

And, just for the record, I did it again. In the paragraph above, I spelled enamored, "enamoured", which was highlighted by my spell-checker, and when I looked it up found this was an accepted spelling elsewhere, unlike the correct American spelling, "enamored". Although this is not proof of anything, it is certainly interesting food for thought.

PURPOSE

If there is a creator, a purpose, and an order; if there is progression, there must be a spiritual truth with values. Otherwise there would only be randomness and chaos. There would be no such thing as progression or learning lessons. In the absence of spiritual truth, lessons would be irrelevant or extraneous.

There must be inviolable spiritual values which we seek to learn and incorporate into our existence, knowledge, and behavior. Among those core spiritual values there must be room for an infinite number of underlying choices and preferences. Otherwise there would be no possibility of individuality, freedom, and free will. We would all be automatons.

So there must be a fine network of absolute truths with many underlying subsets of individual preferences and alternatives.

My suspicion is that the greatest ultimate principle is love, the choice not to intentionally harm others, to do to them as we desire to be done unto, to act in kindness, compassion, and beneficence. Free will permits us to act otherwise and to allow negativity and harm to exist, but I believe that is why we are on earth learning - to not make those choices and to feel the consequences of those choices to ourselves and others.

Shanna Spalding St. Clair channels, "We each have a God-given intent or purpose." We are also given freedom to choose various avenues of development, both in the afterlife, and in any given incarnation.

ENLIGHTENMENT

Enlightenment is a process accomplished over many incarnations, and it is our general purpose. Within that general purpose, we each have individual missions and destinies, part of which is our God-given intent, and part of which is originated and shaped by us.

Gretchen Vogel writes, "Death is not the ticket to enlightenment. That must happen in life if at all." The simple act of dying does not impart super human wisdom. That is a cumulative process directed by us in cooperation with our Creator.

ULTIMATE DESTINY

I have asked many times whether when we reunite with Source we have our individual identity obliterated or whether we remain individuals. The most informative answer I have heard I read in Shanna Spalding St. Clair's channeled book, "We become individualized parts of the whole with no need for expression in form. On the seventh plane, God's laws become individualized. Interests become more personal."

That would seem to indicate that we retain a selfhood, that we keep an individual directing consciousness, with individual interests and purpose.

Although the idea of an eternal rest or a sublime, contemplative state, or obliteration of selfhood and individuality may be appealing to some, I take comfort in the notion that my ultimate destiny may still involve a "me", that my identity, thoughts, and feelings may remain intact, albeit, existing and working in concert with my Creator.

PART III

OBSERVATION AND SPECULATION

SHARED HUMAN/SPIRIT MENTAL EXPERIENCES

Are the mental experiences that humans (spirits in the body) and spirits out of the body create together real? Do spirits actually participate in events with us?

I was recently at a spirit circle and there was a very interesting reading that one of the mediums gave to another who had lost their spouse and was bereaved. The medium said, "Do you still ride the motorcycle?" The recipient of the message said "No, I don't ride anymore." And the medium replied, "Well, she's telling me that you do and that she's with you." And with that the recipient said, "Well, in my mind I do and we're always together." The medium then replied, "Well, you were actually doing it. Even though it's in your thoughts, it's real. You actually are doing it together when you both think it."

This exchange made me think of the many times my partner in spirit has been accompanying me on trips, to work, to mediumship seminars, to parties, as well as all the commonplace events and nuances of my life.

The first medium who brought us together after my partner passed, Robert Brown, told me that we are together now. I thought of all the things that we have done or fantasized doing together, one of which is ballroom dancing. Interestingly enough, in one of the readings a medium gave me, my partner mentioned twirling me around on the ballroom floor. We have both simultaneously visualized doing it together, so perhaps in both of our imaginations as we do it together, we are actually doing it, because our mutual thoughts and mutual agreement make it real.

Maybe you've experienced this, that when you think of one thing it often sets off a chain reaction, which makes you think of another thing, then another thing, all of these thoughts related. As I thought of how real our thoughts together are, I remembered what a dear friend, a priest named Dr. Fehring, told me when I was 18 years old and in college. He told me to be careful what you think because thoughts are things in another dimension of reality. I also recall a passage in the Bible stating that if a man looks at a woman to lust for her he has already committed adultery with her in his heart. This quotation emphasizes that we often underestimate the importance of thought.

Suddenly all of these things came together and I realize that when two people are in agreement and share the same mental experiences they are in effect really doing these things together just as much as they would be if they were doing them together physically. That is why deliberate and strongly expressed intentions are so powerful.

As the physical dimension is the more evanescent, and all physical things pass, but the spiritual dimension is eternal, I have concluded that the things that we think of that we agree on, that we imagine, that we mutually share in our thoughts are as real if not more so than those performed in the physical.

ARE SOULS HAPPIER IN THE AFTERLIFE OR ON EARTH?

My guide indicates, "It depends on the soul. It takes time to get adjusted and some don't want to adjust.

Some aren't ready to come over, love their family, or want to stay on earth. It depends on how they died. It depends on the soul and how they feel about their own life and death. Some have unfinished business or attachments to people, objects, or places. Some have resentments or anger at injustice. Some are reluctant to go because they have fear of retribution for negative acts they committed in their lifetime. Some are very happy to go if they have been suffering a long time. There are some who don't want to go and some who do.

They are all different. No one has the same story. People usually prefer to stay in the body until they finish their work. People may have a deep desire to help their families and wish they were there to live out their lives. It's so difficult because no one feels identically. No single answer fits all."

WHAT ACCOUNTS FOR PERSONALITY CHANGES IN PEOPLE?

What accounts for abrupt changes of personality in people? Which is the real them, one, the other, or both?

I had a close relative who underwent a dramatic shift in personality, and I wondered about this. Was he the man I had known before or the one he became, who was totally different? Had he been lying or concealing who he was earlier, was he both, or now changed?

I know that there are various causes of personality change – dementia, organic and chemical imbalances, substance abuse, emotional trauma, and value or attitude changes. I never got a clear answer. I do know the person he became was not the person he was. I saw several possible candidates for this change.

One was that he had a medical mishap in which a nurse gave him an inappropriate medication and dose, and caused his blood pressure to plummet until he was unconscious. After that incident there was an abrupt and permanent change in his mentation and thought patterns. He was no longer the person I had known. I suspect ischemia secondary to severely low pressure with subsequent brain damage.

After this he began to drink alcohol inappropriately, which added to the problem — now there was substance abuse. In addition, he had a malevolent caregiver, who attempted to induce him to take alcohol, illegal drugs, and tobacco.

He also then underwent a spiritual shift from having attended church with positive behavior, to no interest in spiritual activities, to substance abuse, demeaning comments, insults, drunkenness, and stating that he had lied to me all along. He also became inconsiderate, unfeeling and cruel.

This was a complete about face. In this instance I think the change was multi-factorial, starting with brain damage from the medical mishap, exacerbated by a malicious caregiver and subsequent substance abuse, which triggered a departure from spiritual values to a full onset of negative and abusive comments and behavior. Basically, the person I had known was gone, replaced by another person I didn't know, one who was uncaring, abusive and unloving.

I was truly disturbed because he was one person I trusted in my lifetime and one I could count on. I would hate to think that my opinions had been that far off. I happened to be talking on the phone one day with a friend who is a medium and while we were talking about some of the issues in our lives, the subject of complex relationships came up. She said he downloaded a lot of information to her and told her his disease process was advanced and affecting his brain. It was such a comfort to know that the kind, compassionate man I had known who was always ready to help others and to give good advice was the man he really was, not the insensitive and seemingly uncaring person I saw in his last days. I had already been troubled by duplicitous people and had trust issues and this final one was like the straw that broke the camel's back. It was such a relief to have resolution from the afterlife that he was indeed sincere and the warm, caring individual I had always believed he was.

I feel that on the other side souls become lucid and aware of their thoughts and actions and their effects, no longer clouded by a physical deficit, substance abuse, and can evaluate spiritual decisions more accurately. At any rate, I feel that judgment is clearer on the other side and such mysteries will be unraveled.

WHY DO SOME SOULS HAVE WORSE TEMPERS?

Why is it that some souls have worse tempers than others or do more harm to other people? Are all souls the same when they are created? Are the differences due to inherent personality differences or to environment – what happened to them?

My guide states, "Inherent personality, weakness, choices, what happened to them, all influence the outcome. Souls can learn to choose more positive responses. This is affected by the personality, level of knowledge and understanding, free will, and their inner strength. They can learn to be more positive, become more knowledgeable, and develop their inner strength to resist negativity. Their inherent personality also plays a part. Some souls may be more inclined to choose more negative options based upon their personality characteristics. If weak or impressionable, or under the influence of mind altering substances, people can be influenced by others, either in the physical or spiritual dimension. We all have different inherent strengths and weaknesses based upon our personalities that are fine-tuned by our level of development.

Inherent nature or disposition, previous experiences, level of development, all influence and blend to shape the nature/personality, which, in turn, dictates our choices and actions."

WHY DO PEOPLE ACT WITH CRUELTY?

My guide communicates, "Some people act against others because they have concern eroded by past injustices and injuries enacted upon them. Some people harm others out of anger, some out of ignorance or unawareness, and some enjoy cruelty. There can be many different factors influencing our choices."

WHAT ABOUT JUSTICE, BREAKING THE LAW, AND CAPITAL PUNISHMENT?

When someone has harmed you deeply, affected your life profoundly and negatively, acted with violence, unscrupulous or vicious behavior, taken the life of a loved one, it is common to feel bitterness, anger, and rage. I believe it takes a person of saintly character to forgive heinous acts, to not desire retribution.

I do not profess to be such a saintly person. I do not know how or if a person in the flesh can find peace if they are the victim of such an act. It is true that vengeance will not bring back what someone has lost. I do believe in karma, that one eventually — sooner or later — has to face the consequences of their deeds. What happens after death to souls who perpetrate evil is unknown to us. I do believe that those who act in heartless cruelty and violence against innocent victims should be removed from society and prevented from continuing to harm others.

History shows that in a majority of cases such sociopaths are not rehabilitated. Whether or not capital punishment or lifetime incarceration is the answer I don't know. Whether society owes it to or is obligated to show mercy to someone who has shown no mercy to others, or to pay for their upkeep for a lifetime is a matter of debate. I understand the argument that humans should not desire to take a life, but has a serial killer or mass murderer lost their privilege to live in the flesh because of their vile deeds? Perhaps I will find a clearer answer to that question on the other side.

DEMONS? NO DEMONS? GOING, 1,2,3.

There are so many spiritual absolutes out there, no wonder everyone is either going crazy or thinks everyone else is. Some individuals report harrowing encounters with negative, non-human entities. Priests and demonologists exorcise demons from people. Are they all liars? Some people have communication or a relationship with God. Are they delusional? Others are certain there is no God, no life after death, and this is all you get. Are they cynical?

There are so many opinions, I find it unbelievable that we aren't all confused. The answer for each of us lies in our soul, that is, if you believe you have one, and if you don't, perhaps it lies in another part of your anatomy.

Well, I have an acquaintance who doesn't believe in demons, another who does but doesn't want to give them power, so doesn't acknowledge them, and another who does believe in them.

As a rose by any other name is just as sweet, I don't think that demons are the only negative entities. Some people, such as serial torturers and killers, seem to give the demons a run for their money.

But, more seriously, I don't agree with some authors, who say there is no such thing as good or evil. Perhaps, this may be because they or their loved ones haven't been tortured and killed yet. Maybe they, themselves, their children, or families have never suffered violence. Would they believe in evil if it touched them, their home, or someone they loved?

I believe that if there is any meaning or purpose to life at all, there are ways I would not like to be treated, and that there are acts and behaviors that are kind or cruel, helpful or malicious, positive or negative. If we're here on earth to learn something, why bother if nothing means anything? Let's have anarchy, and murder, kill, steal, rape, lie, mutilate and destroy others without remorse, with equanimity. No reason not to if there's no good or bad. Imagine if a D.A. said such a thing. Perhaps one has.

If I'm here learning all these lessons for nothing, what a waste. Being a wicked, uncaring, unjust, exploitive person seems easy for some, but being a kind, generous, helpful, unselfish, forgiving person is hard. Fighting selfishness and temptation is difficult. Learning restraint and humility, kindness and charity are work. But if there are no higher ideals, no better ways of relationships and living together than violence and assault, harmfulness and ignorance, what is the true value of life and living? Would it be pleasant to live in such as world? Many people don't think so if they're on the receiving end of the insults. Many of course find it fine to do the giving and harming, as many families protect murderers and felons as long as they aren't the ones abused, as long as it is someone else.

I know that I would not want to live in a world without love. That is a personal decision for each of us.

I have experienced negative treatment at the hands of as others, as well as positive. I have experienced malicious, deliberately harmful people as well as loving, giving people.

PRUDENCE ANN SMITH MD

I do believe in spiritual wickedness, manifested in humans, and in non-human spiritual beings, whatever you want to call them. I believe we as humans can be influenced by both. Since I opened up spiritually, I began to notice an occasional thought that would come through my mind that was totally uncharacteristic of me, something I would never have said, that would be insulting or negative. Sometimes the thought was expressed in words that just "popped into my mind", words I had heard before but had never used and thoughts that were not anything I truly believed in my heart. This troubled me. I wondered where are they coming from? I would never have even thought of such a thing before.

One night I got my answer. I had been depressed over an issue in my life, and in the dream state I clearly heard the words, "Why don't you kill yourself?" I knew that didn't come from me at all. I then recognized that I had failed to set boundaries in one area of my life - the spiritual. I always opened up spirit circles with a prayer for protection but had failed to announce or set boundaries in my mental and personal life.

I did so immediately, stating that no negative thoughts, entities, energies, were welcome in my thoughts, home or life. They are barred out, and only souls and energies at the vibration of the white light and of love are welcome. I said this with feeling and meant it. That dream never came back. I know that it was from some negative entity or spirit. From now on I am careful to set boundaries and make statements concerning my choices and to reject negative spirits and entities. I do this daily.

I can pray for them, but do not welcome them or their influence in my life. I know they're real. They are always present, may always try you, but I invoke the power of our Creator and Source and set up personal boundaries to reject their influence.

We can draw experiences, both negative and positive, to us with our behavior, intentions, and interests. Just as they say you are what you eat, or GIGO, garbage in-garbage out about computers, what we concentrate on, watch, read, and practice can influence us. Our thoughts are sacred to us and should be treated as such.

Our reality is our personal experience. We can learn vicariously, read about something or hear someone's testimony, but the clearest and most powerful memories come from our own experiences. Each of us has our individual databank, which is real and valid to us. Each of us reacts to and interprets our experiences differently. So we must make our own choices and decisions and find our own unique peace and happiness, suited to our own character, without seeking to harm others.

Part of maintaining our mental integrity involves setting up spiritual safeguards, praying before opening up, and shutting down appropriately, as well as elaborating our convictions and establishing ground rules. Just as surely as we wash our clothes and lock our doors, we should protect our most valuable asset, our minds and thoughts, against the intrusion and influence of negative entities by praying, asking guides, loved ones, angels, religious figures, and our Creator for help on a regular basis to evict negative energies from our lives.

TIME TRAVEL – PAST AND FUTURE

Some writers say they can astral travel into the past and future. What does this mean? Do they travel into the actual past or a record of the past? What about the future if we have free will?

It means we can look at the past, re-live it. We can conjecture other outcomes. We can hypothesize other consequences if we had made different decisions. We can't change it. By changing it we would be changing the outcome and karma for those who participated and interacted with us. That would not be allowed, as we would be changing the destiny of others without their consent.

Let's say we decided we wanted to go back and marry a different spouse. We would be changing the path as well as negating the earth lives of any children born from that marriage. That would affect many other people and is not permissible. We can replay or re-live what already occurred or experiment with various possible scenarios, but we cannot alter or change what happened.

If there is something we missed in our lifetime that is highly significant to us or crucial to our forward progression, that may be made possible to us to experience that circumstance, relationship, or event in the afterlife if it is integral to our development and progression as a soul.

In regard to the future, sometimes we set in motion plans and intentions that affect our future. These are subject to change as we have free will. We project into the future as to what will happen based upon the set of intentions and circumstances that are in place now and we see the likely or probable events and consequences of those current circumstances, which include our current situation and the set of human intentions in place.

There are options but also probabilities. Some things are pre-planned by God or us and cannot be changed. Some things we have previously chosen to experience as souls while on our earth journey. Other events are open to change and changing our behavior can alter those consequences. Some are not very flexible and some are flexible. We can alter some. Some we cannot. Those are facets of our lives that are meant to be.

Our thoughts and intentions intersect and interact with those of others as well as the prevailing environment. My answer is that no, some things cannot be changed, but many can.

We see what the likely outcome of the current circumstances will be. Some things are meant to happen. Some things are likely to happen. Based upon the thoughts, ideas, and intentions of others, and on the surrounding environment and circumstances, we can follow these contributing factors and see the likely outcome in the future.

Some aspects of this can be altered by our different choices, actions, and decisions. We are viewing the outcome or result of a set of current probabilities and circumstances. It is like a web of many different inputs from many different people and our various thoughts and actions. It is a complex set of variables and interwoven interactions.

When we change our thoughts and behavior patterns we are altering the future at that point. We can tap into the likely future at any given moment.

There is much more freedom of choice, almost a liquidity in the afterlife. Circumstances are more changeable, and pre-planned courses of learning, or set circumstances required for soul growth and lessons are not as fixed as they are on earth. The afterlife is not structured with as rigid or fixed conditions as those designed and set for learning purposes on earth.

TRUTH AND IMPERFECT PEOPLE, IMPERFECT MEDIUMS

There is a reference in the Bible, "He that is without sin among you, let him cast the first stone at her." Sometimes the same idea is captured in the proverb, "Those who live in glass houses shouldn't throw stones." I'm not perfect, nor is any other person I've met, including my closest loved ones. I believe that our Creator, or Source, is perfect.

If we're not perfect, how can our works, our books, our ideas be perfect? So many of the books I read have contradictory statements. Some statements, even within the same book, are contradictory. One of those is the comment that sometimes the death of a loved one is planned as a life lesson, or challenge for those left behind. Some books express this concept. One that I read indicated that spirit does not impose harsh lessons on us arbitrarily such as that one, but went on later in the same book to state that the death of a loved one can be inevitable and part of our life path, as when that author indicated that he was given foreknowledge of the death of someone before it happened but was forbidden by spirit and guides to tell the associated family, as that death was preplanned in the afterlife and could not be avoided or changed.

PRUDENCE ANN SMITH MD

I believe that some of these events are preplanned for our life lessons, but not in a sense of cold, unfeeling judgments, or harsh punishments. One such case is the basis of the book, "*On the Death of my Son*", by Jasper Swain. That book was particularly poignant to me, as it depicted a love so great that the soul who came into the world as his son loved his father so much that he agreed to die as a young man, to have his life cut short, knowing that his death would profoundly change his father and ultimately turn his father's life around in a spiritual direction and result in his father's soul growth.

This is so moving to me because I have undergone a similar experience. Painful and tragic as it was, I would never have changed my life so completely and in the ways I did if it hadn't happened. Many of our most profound lessons and changes come out of pain or grief. It is said that love is one of the most powerful forces in the universe, providing the impetus for great change. It doesn't mean that we're happy to undergo such devastating events, but it means that trying to take something negative and bring something positive from it, trying to create something of love rather than of failure or defeat and negativity is part of our spiritual growth.

This is similar to a story an acquaintance told me many years ago of his brother and another man he knew. Both men had similar accidents and injuries, in which each had lost a leg. This man's brother went on to substance abuse and died alone, in poverty. The other man went on to live despite his handicap and ended up being a one-legged skier, helicopter skiing from the top of a high mountain. Each faced his challenge differently – one positively, and one negatively.

I bring up these stories to say that when I first started reading voraciously about the afterlife, I encountered many contradictions in the books I read. At first, this bothered me. I questioned myself, what is right and what is wrong? I figured that, in comparison with other professional or more experienced mediums, they must be the experts, and I must somehow have it wrong. After time and thought, I came up with my own answers. In fact, after reviewing some of the statements others have made and comparing them with my own experiences, observations, and discussions with spirit, I have made a complete about-face. I have learned to trust spirit and myself. I have come to my own conclusions and accept my own truth, especially in matters that are extremely important to me. Why let others dictate issues that are closest to my heart? If I'm wrong I have no one but myself to blame.

But I have learned that not all things in life can be known rationally or proven empirically. Some things involve trust. And some things are strong convictions in my heart. I may never have proof for these while I am in a physical body, but perhaps certain things are meant to be so. Strangely, several of these I am more certain of than all the outward facts that can be measured, weighed, or calculated. It's a knowing inside that is beyond anything the rational mind can fathom.

I realized that, as none of us is perfect as a human being, mediums, who are also human beings, are not perfect either. If we can't get communication straight between each other, who can see each other in the physical world, (think of the telephone game, and how statements get twisted before they get to the final recipient), how much more difficult is it to get things accurately from spirit, through another dimension and the mind of the medium, with their own opinions and thoughts? It is so difficult to get information objectively without prejudicing it with our own belief systems or trying to fill in the blanks.

One young medium at a seminar I attended, when given an image of a rifle by my loved one in spirit, supplied with her own mind that he was a hunter, rather than that he was in the service, as he was trying to communicate to her. Another professional, experienced medium, giving me a message in a teaching seminar, told me my aunt was a horticulturist, genetically breeding plants and flowers. My aunt was an avid gardener, but that medium's mind had taken it a step farther and made her a horticulturist. Even professional mediums can try to help the spirit by supplying information with their own mind.

That's why they say, "Give what you get. Don't embellish."

Another reason for contradictions is that none of us has all the spiritual truth. Each of us is at a different level of spiritual development, and we can only give what we have. If we are teaching a subject we can only teach what we ourselves have learned. None of us is an ultimate expert. We have to bear in mind that that particular medium, or that particular spirit communicating through the medium, can only give information of which they are aware, and understanding commensurate with their level of spiritual development.

I have been told, myself, and heard from other mediums that souls do not become perfect or all-knowing, omniscient beings when they die. If someone was unlearned or unskilled in a particular area, they will not instantly turn into an expert in that regard when they die. They can learn or develop those abilities, much as we do on earth, but do not have instant expertise or knowledge in them.

Another reason why contradictions can occur is because many things in life aren't black or white, but there are many opinions, options, beliefs, and realities. On earth we share a diversity of environments, lifestyles, attitudes, faiths, goals and life choices. If you ask one person their opinion about marriage relations, kids, love, ambitions, career, goals, preferences, religious beliefs, or anything else, for that matter, you'll get an answer that is entirely different from that you will get from another person. We're all different and so are our lives.

On the other side we don't change into cookie cutter clones (although I actually had one young medium in training tell me this at a seminar). If we didn't remain individuals, what would the purpose be in being individuals in the first place? If we ceased to be individuals, our own purpose in life would be negated, irrelevant, and what would be the need to undergo lessons to learn if those lessons were made of no effect because we ceased to be the person we were and we were no longer an individual? If we were no longer individuals, what would be the purpose of learning or growth? We wouldn't need it if we didn't remember who we were or what we learned.

I am no longer troubled by the discrepancies I see in the books, realizing these causes, and I now embrace what one medium told me and what I read in one of Charlotte Dresser's books. The medium said I had to find my own truth. The book said, "The afterlife is vast, with room for many truths and realities. Embrace your own truth, and that is the truth you will experience. It is the one that is right for you. Never doubt you shall have it."

That statement is a gem I carry in my heart and pull out for review every time a medium tells me I will no longer care about my loved ones when I die as I did on earth, or that I'll be just as close to some people who made my life miserable as to those who made me glad to be alive, or that I'll cease playing the part I played in this life and no longer be me, my cherished ideals gone, a mindless indistinct generic copy of a soul, indistinguishable from millions of others. It may be difficult to believe, but I have actually been told these things, by mediums who tried to make them sound good and inviting. Maybe it was for them, and hopefully they will enjoy living their reality that they so ardently tried to impose on me. I, however, don't plan on going to their Heaven, but to my own, filled with people who think like me and also cherish the things so dear to me.

I have concluded that on earth there are many lifestyles that would not appeal to any one of us, and each of us seeks out the lifestyle that makes us happy to the best of our ability. There are so many choices of careers, partners, faiths, places to live. Why should that be any less true in the afterlife? If anything, it is more so, with many different dimensions, habitats, and realities, probably more than either you or I could imagine. The only restriction I have ever heard is that we not desire to harm other souls or to act in a manner inconsistent with love. What makes someone else happy would not make you or me happy. We find our own happiness with others of like thinking and mind, if we wish, as it should be. What a prison without walls to be forced to endure another's choice of lifestyle that is not ours.

If God is love, as I believe, God would not want us to be so miserable.

Furthermore, when we relinquish our own choices and power to another, we are surrendering our own freedom and free will as individuals to seek the happiness and fulfillment of our own lives and journeys. The results of our own actions in terms of happiness or sorrow must rest with us. Surely role models and good advice can be good, but ultimately the decision must be ours. Then we have no one but ourselves to blame if we exercise poor judgment. But perhaps that is what poor judgment is for. Experiencing the consequences of our poor judgment is sometimes the only way we learn to make better choices and exercise better judgment.

I learned this when I had a health problem several years ago. I knew I would need a surgery to correct it. I had been a person who often gave in to the will of others during my lifetime for the sake of harmony and peace. This was an error on my part. In this case, I accepted unsolicited advice from a medium and pressure from someone in my life to go ahead with the operation, despite my inner conviction that I should not do it at that time. I didn't listen to the inner voice, but allowed the pressure of others to dictate what I did. I don't blame them for what happened. How could they know a medical error would occur? I do blame myself for allowing others to tell me what to do. I think this was a life's lesson for me.

While I was unconscious during the surgery, I was allowed to aspirate, and, as a result, got lung damage, which resulted in severe bronchitis when I awoke, followed by hours on my feet in respiratory distress immediately after the surgery, thinking I would not live through it. This developed into severe asthma, now followed by three horrible episodes of severe life threatening asthmatic bronchitis this year alone, during one of which I almost died. This occurred because of letting the pressure from others usurp my own better judgment. My quality of life is now severely comprised because of it.

Those who were telling me what to do were well meaning, but I let them dictate my fate, rather than myself, and now have a chronic unfixable problem the rest of my life that will never go away, an illness far more severe than the one I was getting surgery to correct. Never surrender your own judgment to that of someone else or let them determine your fate, however well- meaning. Your decisions and outcome should be your own. LESSON LEARNED.

In the same manner, when you read something in a book that is contradictory, including this one, or something that does not resonate with you, discard it. Ignore it. Choose your own truth, because that is ultimately the one on which you will stand or fall, the one that is right for you. And, as we are all learning, when or if that truth no longer serves your greatest good or highest purpose, change it. Evolve. Grow. Learn. Become the better, wiser, more loving soul you, I, and all others are meant to be.

Kelvin Cruikshank, a New Zealand Medium, and author of the book, "*Finding the Path*", states, "In silence we can know spirit – truly know, through our own experience, rather than hearing someone else's version."

LESSONS, JUSTICE, AND PURPOSE

Are murders and tragedies of life planned beforehand in the afterlife?

Since souls are regarded as planning the major points of their lives and deaths in the afterlife, to what extent are murders and tragic deaths planned? Do souls know they will be victims of foul play or tragic circumstances before they arrive?

I've been told that although a murder or tragic ending can occasionally be planned or experienced by a soul, that this is rare, and as we all have free will, is usually the result of bad decisions on the part of those involved, rather than an intended outcome.

Authors have indicated that we are not to blame God for wars or the cruelties imposed by some human beings on others. Why does God permit this to occur? Because God has given us free will, we don't live in a police state, and the origin of these acts is man's inhumanity to his fellow man.

As far as the concept of instant forgiveness on the part of victims, instant transformation of those who act in an evil manner into good, or instant healing, these are not set in stone, and souls transitioning to the other side react as differently as we do on earth. Some find it easy to forgive the perpetrators and others are bitter, angry, or seek justice. They are not happy at their tragic or violent endings, can become upset, agitated, fearful at reliving the circumstances of their death, and do not blissfully forget them. Some need much healing.

Others, although capable of working through the issues and coming to a point of forgiveness, often desire to have their story told and the truth come out. Some even remain very negative or cynical when they cross, poisoned by the circumstances and relationships of their lives, perhaps unable to see that they even had other choices, feeling condemned by fate. Some even wish to continue in negative behavior or drug use if they could, while some would even seek to harm the innocent or those who desire to help them, becoming in an ironic way like the perpetrators who hurt them, turning and desiring to act like those predators and hurt others who are innocent as they themselves were hurt.

I am assuming that some of these who become or remain negative after death have not crossed to the other side where they might receive help with those issues, see things from a larger perspective, or be prevented from desiring to harm others or continue in destructive behavior.

All souls do not seem to be equally happy in the afterlife, depending on whether their lives were fulfilled or upon their degree of materialistic thought, development, and the main focus of their desires on earth, whether selfish, materialistic, and violent, or unselfish, spiritual, and benevolent.

There seem to be many levels of development in the afterlife, many individual perspectives, just as on earth. If all were instantly transformed into all-knowing, idyllic, angelic beings, we would have no need for lessons, life reviews, continued reincarnations, levels and progression and learning.

Lessons are difficult at best, even for those of us on earth who have a greater understanding or who are kinder, less selfish, and better behaved. The upward climb is just that, not a pole vault into Heaven, so to speak, but a gradual progression.

We remain individuals on the other side with tendencies and traits like we had on earth and often battle to change the worst of these or to gain enlightenment. Spiritual growth does not come easy and exacts the price of patience, tolerance, effort, and fortitude. I remember reading a child's book when I was young called, *"A Magic Word for Ellen"*. That word was SISU, and meant courage, determination, and fortitude. We all need these in our upward climb.

Another thing I have learned by reading extensively is that there are many ideals and individual values, points of view that persist in the afterlife. Not all agree upon or desire the same thing any more than they did on earth. This is not necessary. Death does not transform us into clones or a race of zombies. We retain individual identity, differences, and perspective.

However, life is meant to teach us to be kind, tolerant of differences, patient, forgiving, helpful, merciful, and understanding; above all, to learn to desire to help others rather than to harm or do violence to others. We are meant to learn to respect one another and treat each other with kindness, as we ourselves wish to be treated.

Those are the lessons to which we are meant to aspire. We have no time limit to attain them. But these principles lead to happiness, while violence against others, selfishness, exploitation, abuse, or harm do not. In the veiled atmosphere of earth, in which true motives can be hidden and atrocities committed against others are often unrevealed, in which crimes often go unsolved or unpunished and there is seemingly so little justice, yet karma persists inevitably. So little of the spiritual consequences of their actions is known to many people. They often feel themselves above justice or never needing to answer for their deeds- until they get to the other side and realize it is real.

Every word, thought and deed we commit is preserved in the Akashic records, and, as such, compels a reaction or response, whether good or bad. Justice is in our hands and we create the judgment ourselves. That is like a law of action and reaction. By our choices we create our own karma or future circumstances. By our own choices we can change it.

We have free will and are learning to act and choose responsibly.

Negative Baggage, Spiders' Webs

My guide gave me an image or analogy for the baggage we can carry with us from the past. He compared it to spider's webs, indicating that although we can easily break the fibers of a spider's web, we may see them as confining or trapping us, or as sticky strands that are hard to remove from us.

I walked around with those webs on me for a while and know how difficult they can be to remove. Especially when we have been caught in repetitive negative patterns throughout our lifetime, they can become entrenched like a bad habit, and hard to break.

They cause all kinds of problems. They can change our self-image, our self-esteem. I had experienced a loss of self-worth because of allowing others to take advantage of me and in some instances to denounce me or abuse me verbally. I let the criticism erode my own sense of value or worth as a human being, expecting to be treated like that because I no longer saw myself as being worthy of respect or dignity. They also changed my outlook on other people, no longer trusting others, and my opinion of humanity plummeted. These feelings engendered a larger sense of bitterness, cynicism, and disappointment, and culminated in depression.

I didn't know how to release the baggage. It was ultimately love, respect and caring that released me. But it didn't happen overnight.

PRUDENCE ANN SMITH MD

I had to grow to accept that I was worthy of kind treatment and respect. I then had to learn how to trust again, to trust my loved one, that I no longer had to wait for the axe to fall, for all that was good to disappear, and the carpet to be pulled out from underneath me. And then I had to recognize that there is love, that not all humanity is predatory, out to lie, abuse or use others. That good had to become real to me, not just witnessed second hand on the internet or described by other people in positive relationships.

I had to understand what happened to me before I could take steps to change it, understand why it happened, what lesson I was meant to learn, and find out what part I played in permitting it to happen, as well as what I should do the next time it occurred. This was a process, not just an epiphany.

It took time to heal, change my thought, and then change my behavior. I realized that until you stop it and are prepared to suffer whatever consequences there are, it will not stop. That was when I learned that you have to be assertive when you are on the receiving end of negativity. I once would have used the word, "victim", but no longer see myself as a victim, but rather as a person who has now learned a lesson, that when I am able to prevent it, I will not accept negative or abusive treatment.

All learning and change takes effort, but as I realize the results in my life, I know that the effort was worth it, becoming a happier person, freed from the bondage of old insults, stronger, no longer able to be intimidated by aggressive, abusive people, no longer buying into the behavior that destroys my sense of personal value, and with more peace in my heart.

LEARNING LESSONS TOGETHER

I have read and been told that we learn lessons here on the earth as well as on the other side. In fact, I understand that we can learn them together. We never cease learning.

I know that we can be inspired by those on the other side, guides, loved ones, or even influenced by those who are negative if we don't protect ourselves and are open to their influence.

But I understand that those on the other side who have had similar life's problems to ours can observe the way we handle similar situations and learn from us. Likewise, we often have guides who have already learned from situations like the ones we confront, and can help support or inspire us in our attempt to learn similar lessons. Where do those who have problems with alcohol go? To others who have overcome the same problems.

I recently became aware of a similar learning situation in my own life. Overcoming emotional scars from negative situations in our lives is an arduous task. My loved one in spirit has acted very patiently as my guardian and guide, accompanying me through seemingly endless repeated attempts to heal from past hurts. He has stood by me, unflagging, and given me advice and help. How anyone would not have given up on me from sheer exhaustion I don't know.

But there was a problem. Because of the past trauma my emotional state was such that I was unable to fully receive what he was telling me. All the encouragement in the world could not help me unless I was able to believe in myself. Finally, I reached the point where I was confident enough to believe in myself and what he was saying. At last I was mentally and emotionally able to receive and benefit from those messages. I asked him to give them to me one more time. He opened his heart and did so.

That was the moment in which I was healed of the past hurts and trauma to the point where I could move on and let the burden go.

I already had all the information I needed. Why make it more difficult? I saw I needed to open my heart, too, and let certain things which weren't that important go. I realized that I had to finally stand up and let the past be where it was – in the past, and not relive scenarios daily.

Overcoming emotional trauma is a process, and working on our issues with the help and support of our loved ones, whether in the body or in spirit, is a complex dance. It is a marriage of give and take, requiring sensitivity and patience. I am very thankful for my loved one's willingness to open his heart and compromise in order to help me overcome the burdens. I learned that love is demonstrated by giving and compromising, by helping one another. What he did made a significant difference in my future and my life. I thank him for that kindness, those concessions, that gift that means so much to me in my journey. He also is an example to me of what I can be, what I will be for him when he needs my help, as I needed his.

Referring to healing, Kelvin Cruikshank, in his book, *"Finding then Path,"* discusses healing and states "Words set everything free. There is nothing worse than a secret – and it's pointless trying to hide the truth because it will always come out."

THE MANY MANSIONS OF THE AFTERLIFE

As each of us would give a different answer if we were asked questions about love, justice, right and wrong, God, relationships, priorities and values, so spirits would each have their own beliefs and opinions. At least on the earth plane and similar levels in the afterlife, no one universal truth is held by all. Souls still have different values and opinions.

Look at the different comments given by mediums. Some say it is perfectly safe to channel spirits and others say it is dangerous. These differences may be accounted for by personal beliefs or experiences.

At any rate, the afterlife is even more diverse than the earth, and what is one soul's experience and preference is not that of another. What is right for one is certainly not right for all. What would make one happy would not make another happy. We don't even have to look beyond our own family and friends to see that. What I want is quite different from what others want, even my own friends with whom I share many things in common.

Therefore, many of the apparently dissimilar things in the afterlife are just alternatives, options, normal variability that souls can choose and experience. If there were only one way, one experience, how unhappy many would be. I'm sure that each experiences the reality they prefer.

Answers from the Afterlife

The ultimate values and characteristics of God, I believe, are eternal truths, and I believe that as souls we will become aware of these and incorporate them as we advance.

My friend's guide referred to it as purification – that we become more pure as we progress as souls.

But within that framework, there are, I believe, many realities or environments and choices for us as souls. Some books describe souls as hanging in pods in between lives, and others describe the afterlife as similar to an ideal earth plane. I know they used to say, "Try it, you'll like it," but the pod option just isn't me.

Why must one be right and another wrong? Don't some people on earth live in remote wilderness and others in crowded impoverished conditions, while yet others live in luxury and material wealth? Why not differences on the other side?

What about the many mansions described in the Bible? There might be one just right for you and one for me. I hope so.

DO WE INSTANTLY FORGIVE AND HEAL WHEN WE DIE?

Some mediums paint an idyllic picture of the afterlife and some paint a picture of an idealized earth. As I'm sure there are many different conditions and levels in the afterlife, probably both are correct.

But I've often wondered whether those who have been deeply hurt in their lifetime, those who have suffered tragedies, murder, untimely deaths, are instantly transformed and healed.

I know there are many reports of angry ghosts who carry their similar personalities to the other side. Some are reported to take out their anger on innocent humans who cross their paths. Some were negative while alive, fear judgment, and remain negative after death. Some mediums describe a need to work out problems between souls on the other side.

As there are life reviews we each face, we learn of our original intent and lessons for our recent life, of whether we achieved our goals or not, and feel the pain and reactions we caused others, as they feel the pain and reactions they caused us. It has been said that souls work out their issues, decide what they did right or wrong, and consider alternatives for what they could or should have done.

ANSWERS FROM THE AFTERLIFE

It seems that much healing goes on, on the other side. It has not been indicated to me that forgiveness is instant or automatic, like turning off a light switch. There appears to be a need for discussion, resolution of issues, and forgiveness before the individual souls can move on. Some mediums indicate that spirits who cross over and feel remorse for the way they behaved toward someone on earth seek forgiveness and closure before they can move on.

Since that can happen on earth, how much more so on the other side where we see the bigger picture? Many unanswered questions are answered. Many deceits and lies are cleared up, and at last souls know the truth. It is said that our character and motives are transparent on the other side, that we cannot hide our intentions and true character. It has even been said that history is intriguing on the other side because the real events and motivations are what we discover, not just what is acceptable, sugar-coated, or printed in the history books for public consumption.

What a shock for some and a relief for others.

From what I have been told, there is a great deal of healing and a great deal of resolution and closure needed for some souls. While it takes many lifetimes to change our faults, to attempt to perfect ourselves and progress, why would we be expected to instantly turn into perfected angels when we die, or instantly resolve all conflicts and serious issues of a lifetime with others?

I'm sure that these issues are clearer when we can see the bigger picture and see ourselves and others for who we really are, know what we have truly said and done, not just what is shown to the public. I've been told that some drama persists, some issues bleed over, but that forgiveness is worked on and possible, that differences become hills rather than mountains, and hearts and minds are eventually healed.

Certainly this is easier when we are no longer being provoked, hurt, or abused by someone. They can't hurt us in the afterlife, without a physical existence, without the negative situations that can occur on earth. When you are freed from an abusive situation it is easier to forgive than when you are continuing in one.

But who has real resolution just because someone can't hurt you? Real resolution comes when someone no longer desires or chooses to hurt you. As we carry our innate personalities with us, although there is no longer a need for cultural differences, we are shaped by a combination of our past experiences, which are all unique, making us a unique consciousness and individual linked with all others by our divine spiritual origin and common universal needs, refined and tempered by our own personalities, desires, and characteristic outlooks.

I'm sure that although we honor or respect the best part of each other, as one spirit told me, there are some with more similar personalities, some with more common interests, some with more similar opinions, some with a greater chemistry or affinity. Does everyone match as closely or fit together like a hand in glove? Does everyone have a deep, deep love? Albert, one of the spirits communicating through Matthew Smith, says we go over to those we love. This would imply there are some we do not.

The channeling spirits in Shanna Spalding St. Clair's books, "*Karma I and II*", say there is always a connection between spirits who love one another, implying that some don't, at least not in a personal sense. Kelvin Cruickshank, a New Zealand medium and psychic detective, refers to those we love on the other side and also refers to both negative and positive spirits. I have been told that although those spirits who are positive have a loving kindness for other souls, an appreciation for the lessons we learn from each other, and that we help each other on our journeys, that not all souls are equally compatible or close, that not all share equal bonds of love.

Most mediums say it is our deceased loved ones and relatives who remain close to us, watch over us, and help us through our earthly lives, not strangers, although sometimes angels or strangers have been reported to help others in need. So there certainly are individual ties that persist. Not all souls are connected in a personal sense, but they are in the divine origin of their spirit. So there are personal networks, including souls groups, families, and individual deep bonds of lasting love, and larger universal spiritual networks depicting our similar origin in God or Source.

I know in my heart what is true for me, which may not be what is true for others. This is as it should be, as we are not all the same, and what makes one happy is not what makes another happy. I'm thankful for our diversity and individuality. Why the need for all of us if we were all identical? We each have our own destiny, or own goal, our own future, our own star to aim for. I have mine, and I'm on the path now. I may stumble now and then, but as long as I get back up and head onward, I'll make it wherever I'm supposed to be eventually. And I'm happy in my visions and dreams, busy making them reality, separating the gold from the ore.

PERSONAL LOVE

I have read a medium's statement that there is no retention of personal love on the other side, only a generic love with all souls loving one another perfectly and equally. Why is it that some spirits indicate that they're together and happy if there is no individual or personal love that lasts on the other side? Then Mary, Dick, Jane, Adolph, Bluebeard, and Genghis Khan would be interchangeable. There would be no persistent love or feelings for anyone we have cared about on the earth. Why do family members or loved ones come through to us if there is no abiding love? Then why not strangers? And why do spirits indicate that they are acting as guardian angels for their younger family members if there is no lasting tie of love?

If we were just acting a role when we hurt or killed someone, why is there a need for resolution or forgiveness on the other side if we're just posing and acting out what was supposed to happen? All these suppositions would make learning and growth irrelevant.

And out of the zillions of souls, why would there be any need for continuity of relationships if no personal love remains or exists on the other side, if everyone just loves everyone else equally? Then that abusive ex-husband or child molester uncle will be A-number one on the other side, as equally loved and cherished as the grandchild they molested or the wife they abused. We could affiliate with Hitler, Jeffrey Dahmer, John Wayne Gacy, Jack the Ripper, or BTK, or any other sadistic killer just as easily as our own supposedly beloved grandchild, our cherished husband or wife, our kindly parent. If no distinctions in morality or personality persist, what is the point? What really matters?

Do we really spend equal amounts of time with all the zillions of souls in existence? Do we even know them all? I've heard that certain people met for the first time in the afterlife. Is it possible if we retain individual identity that we are all equally and identically compatible? Is it possible that the deep loves engendered on earth mean nothing on the other side, that we have equal love for a vicious murderer as for someone who was irreplaceable to us while we were alive? Why have relationships like that if they just die, if they are annulled by the gate of death?

Some have said that we have relationships like a branching family tree, some intimate and close, some more distant. Some have said that regarding those with whom we've had incompatible abrasive, turbulent relationships, that we just don't see much of that person on the other side. Some have said former mates in an incompatible marriage, without that small spark of true love, go separate ways, assessing what they have learned from one another. If we retain any uniqueness, any individuality as spirits or souls, although we may respect, honor, and help one another on the other side, there must be something other than just a zombie-like love for one another; there must be some souls more compatible, with a greater affinity for one another. What is individual love and connection worth if it is wiped out by death, if those deep loves we have with some individuals in life don't persist?

Just by the differences in thought, personality, and goals or interests some of us are more attuned to one another than others. If these deep loves are erased or all become generic and identical then we as souls must become cardboard cutouts or holograms, no longer the souls we were. Too many souls coming in from the other side have indicated that they are together, re-united and happy, or watching over their progeny, their loved ones, not some random stranger. Some have said they will be with another soul always. If we all just love one another equally and automatically on the other side, then any one soul can replace another.

Why do some souls say that some couples who were married on earth separate and some remain together? Why is it said that there is such a thing as individual choice and free will if by necessity we must remain with and love all souls equally? Why then do some souls say we "go over to those we love" if we love all the same? That would imply we don't. Why would a teacher from the other side say "there is always a connection between those who love one another even when one is in spirit", if there is no difference in the love we have for souls and no individual love?

If there is no variable depth of love between souls, why would relationships matter, why would they continue? One would be as good as another. Why would soul groups remain together? All would be equanimous. Why would some couples re-unite and some say they will always be together, that they are soul mates or twin flames? Why would some souls say they have been together for eons? It doesn't add up.

Certainly souls respect each other more, as one soul spoke about his former rival, "We honor the best part of one another." Certainly souls see their own errors as well as the bigger picture. Certainly souls are less ego-driven and care for the welfare of others, loving less selfishly. But within this general regard, concern, and helpfulness, the loving kindness described by one medium, there must be a special link, a unique bond between some souls, a like-mindedness, the persistence of a prior good relationship, a special compatibility or affinity, a deeper or more harmonious "oneness", a stronger tie, a greater congeniality or sympathy based on temperament and character.

Someone who has felt that tie with someone could not imagine being separated from that soul, could not imagine a happiness as great with anyone else, could not imagine the same quality of life without that person. For those who love that special soul, joy is in that love, meaning is in that love. Why the possibility of soul unions if no such special love exists? Why the need for any particular companionship if any will do? What is the value of love if it isn't true, if it isn't forever? Is commitment made nothing?

Love is like a magnetic law of attraction and entails concern for the welfare of the other and for happiness with them. A general "Godly" love is an unselfish regard for the welfare of others, but companionship with one with whom we feel an affinity is a gift, a pairing, a union that is different from the general appreciation and caring empathy we can have with all souls.

My guide states, "We have some that we love differently in the afterlife, some more than others in a sense of personal companionship. We do love some more intensely than others, but we also have a love that is expressed as caring, concern, and helpfulness toward all souls, an unselfish love, a beneficent, humanitarian love, which can be described as an all-encompassing spiritual love, a regard for the welfare of others, a collective love.

There is also a unique love between individual compatible souls. It's the love that we have for individuals we care about and want to be with. It's a very deep and intense personal love.

We have deep and unbreakable ties with some souls. There are degrees of love in a personal, individual sense. Love is of the spirit and more lasting based on spiritual compatibility. Those ties determine our closest companions and our most enduring relationships.

The other form of love is non-specific, an unselfish, giving concern for all other souls and their welfare. It is a Godly form of love that is not based on individual compatibilities or how we get along. It is the love of all souls, a Mother Theresa type of love, a non-distinguishing love for the benefit and development of all."

I know I do not want to be become part of some primeval homogenous mush, lose my selfhood, consort with Jack the Ripper, and live on in a blissful mindless existence. I want to cherish, retain, and nurture the deep loves I have known, pursue the future with a sharing, loving companion, both of us just right for one another, and have one rollicking, ecstatic, fulfilling, afterlife, seeking the truth, doing good, and having the closest union two souls can have. And, by gum, if we can create our own future reality, we're busy creating it right now.

THE AFTERLIFE AND QUANTUM PHYSICS

The Popular Notion of Trying to Equate the Afterlife with Quantum Physics

It is now a popular endeavor to make the afterlife conform to the popular theories of quantum physics. The afterlife is more than a limited popular construct of the human mind in the material world.

Although we attempt to understand the afterlife by analogy to our human circumstances and understanding, it cannot be completely explained by reasoning and templates that apply to the physical domain. The laws that govern the physical domain cannot be completely transposed to a non-physical domain that is greater and more complex.

SIMULTANEOUS LIVES, TIME, TIMELESSNESS, AND LEARNING

If we have free will there must of necessity be a future, not just multiple simultaneous lives. Free will automatically implies that we can change the future. So if there is free will there must be a future. If that is the case, we must be able to affect that future with our choices.

If only multiple simultaneous lives existed, we could never learn and grow from our mistakes, change our future, or even have one, for that matter. In order to benefit by learning from our past, there must first be a past, and we must be able to apply what we have previously learned to our decisions in the future. If all we did was live all of our lives simultaneously, we would never be able to apply the learning from our lessons to better decisions in the future.

Also, in order to have soul progression and learning, there must be something to learn in the first place. Otherwise there would be no purpose in our existence. Second, in order to benefit from that learning, there must be a past from which we learn, and a future into which we incorporate better decisions based upon our past learning.

Why do some authors and mediums say there is no time on the other side? This is because there is no time as we know it. Past, present and future still exist, but time in the earthly sense is not significant when we have no bodies that age or decay, no seasons, cycles of light and darkness, no growing of food or need for daily sleep. Time is no longer significant in the demarcation of years or in the cycle of work, eating, and sleep that governs daily earth life. I am told by Spirit that the passage of time does not have the same relevance and that the sense of time we mark with the turn of the planet and orbits, cycles of day, night, seasons and years is not there and awareness of the passage of time becomes unimportant and irrelevant.

INCONSISTENCIES OF THE MULTIPLE SIMULTANEOUS REINCARNATIONAL SELVES THEORY

If you are able to fragment your soul into countless pieces and live every personality and life you will ever live at the same time, who am I to say you can't? If you can live every one of those countless lives with every permutation of choice and detail, causing an infinite number of additional lives based on each subsequent choice and its outcome, like a ripple effect, all at one time, then you must feel very schizophrenic or the victim of multiple simultaneous personality disorder.

If this life is a school filled with lessons and we have a life review when we die to see what we learned so that we can progress and carry our new knowledge over into our next reincarnation so that we can grow, become better people, and make better choices, how is that possible if we're living every lifetime we'll ever have simultaneously? How can we ever learn from our choices in order to do better in the future if there is no sequential future, and all lifetimes are occurring at the same time as we speak? That way we would never benefit from our experience.

ANSWERS FROM THE AFTERLIFE

It is said that we plan our incarnations as a soul group so that each individual benefits from the incarnation and learns their planned and needed lessons. If our lives are all occurring at the same time and we can choose to alter our choices, then we must necessarily and subsequently be altering everyone else's outcomes in the incarnations without their consent. That way we are continually altering history including each other person's personal history, without their consent, including the changed lessons they will have to learn. Or, if we can go back and alter our choices we are then altering other people's paths against their will. What happened to their free will then? But does back even exist if all of our lives are simultaneous? That in itself is a contradictory paradox.

One author who espoused the multiple simultaneous reincarnational selves belief contradicted himself in his own book when he then went on to say that certain moral regimens were outdated because they were antiquated, being from the past and appropriate to those living at that time. What? I thought he just said earlier in the same book there was no past, just multiple simultaneous lives? I couldn't make sense of the multiple simultaneous lives, let alone the contradiction saying that there now is a past and it's outdated currently.

If souls are meant to come across and learn and discuss what they did wrong or could have done better, there must of necessity be a past to discuss, not just ongoing multiple lives. How could we carry our knowledge over into successive lives if there are no successive lives?

Then, when mediums speak of our ancestors helping us from the other side, this would not be possible if they are all living their infinite number of lives at the same time, unless of course we are all living an infinite number of afterlives at once also and we are not one soul, but legion. Then we would have no personal identity, or each of us would have infinite identities at the same time. Who am I? Which one am I today? No, wait a minute. There is no today. There is no tomorrow or yesterday. I am then an infinite number of souls but how can I speak for all those different souls and personalities at once? I think I must have an identity crisis with all these infinite separate identities and I can't speak for any one? Which one should I be today? If this is the case, there is no order, logic, or progression, only chaos.

I don't think I serve a God of chaos. Or are you saying there are an infinite number of gods in an infinite number of universes and they are all as confused as you are?

DEAD OR ALIVE

If we are greeted by loved ones when we die and our separation from our physical body is facilitated by spiritual helpers, how is it possible that some spirits don't realize they're dead? If there is "no coincidence" how can a death not be foreknown?

In a discussion with another medium, different answers were obtained.

First, there are accidental, traumatic deaths, such as battlefield deaths and various sorts of accidents that are unanticipated and fast. These may not allow for the presence of loved ones or helpers, and the person who died unexpectedly, rapidly, and traumatically may not even realize they're dead.

Second, the dying person may have dementia or be of unsound mind, and such mental afflictions may take a while to resolve after death. A friend who is both a medium and a psychologist indicates that she has communicated with some spirits who had addictions in their lifetime and indicated that their quality of thought was affected for a while after their death.

Third, a person's ideology may interfere with their awareness and perception after death. They may be in denial about an afterlife or have strong convictions that predispose them to certain expectations about the afterlife that may influence their experience, as the afterlife is a "mental reality" more readily influenced by our desires and beliefs than the more concrete environment of the earth plane.

Fourth, not all situations are the same. If the person was cruel or had few positive ties with others in life, perhaps no one will show up to "receive" them in death.

Fifth, I have heard from those who have had NDE's and returned to the body that they don't "feel" any different when they leave the body and that they just are free from pain and have a great sense of peace. If someone doesn't believe in the continuation of life after death, they may assume they are still alive if they retain their consciousness and may not realize they have departed until they see their body or realize they can't get back inside the body. This may be especially true for children who don't have a concrete concept of death and may not initially realize they have passed over if they don't feel any different.

All of these possibilities could explain a spirit initially not being aware that they are "dead."

HOW SOON IS TOO SOON?

We were recently asked to give a reading for a professional who was devastated over having lost an associate to a recent suicide. It has been a subject of debate in the mediumship community as to how soon after a loved one's death someone should seek a reading. Different sources give different recommendations.

Some argue that immediately after a loss the sitter is too emotionally distraught and labile to get the most out of a reading. Others say that the spirit needs an adjustment period in the afterlife before they can come through. I don't think there are hard and fast rules. Every person and every spirit is different. One person may be too emotionally impaired to be able to appreciate what is said while another may be able to comprehend and handle the communication. Some spirits are able to come through almost immediately while others can't. It depends on the spirit's emotional state and how well they were able to communicate in their lifetime.

I had had spirits come through almost immediately after their death. Others seem to have to learn how to communicate much as a medium has to practice to get better. Spirits improve in communication with time and practice as we on earth do in almost any endeavor. Some who have been teachers and lawyers and have spent much of their lives talking often have a facility with communicating, and I can often hear them clairaudiently, while communication with other spirits may be more clairvoyant through images.

For that matter, many people have been awakened in the middle of the night to see a vision of their loved one standing at the foot of their bed and know that their loved one has passed and has come to "say goodbye". Of course, this is not really goodbye, only a "see you later". We never lose the ones we love in spirit, as they can still be contacted, despite the absence of a physical body. My friend got a visit from his uncle who had just died, unbeknownst to him, while my friend was in a coma. He heard his uncle's voice assuring him that he would be all right. The only thing was that the uncle had just died when this visit occurred.

One time when I was unable to attend our Skype spirit circle, they assisted the friend of one of the members in making his transition across, communicating with him while he passed. So it seems spirits can communicate while and just after they have passed as well.

I also know that if the sitter has a deep emotional need for the reading, spirits such as guides, teachers, and angels often come together and help the communicating spirit to come through by giving their energy. This is the same shared group energy from the spirit world that facilitates table-tipping and the same shared audience energy that aids in telekinesis and spoon-bending.

When my loved one first communicated with me from the spirit world, I know that there was a contribution of group energy that helped him to come through, as there also was when I was given some teaching and lessons from the other side, including when I was give a 24 hour life-review from my Akashic record that I will never forget. It went on for 24 hours straight and I couldn't turn it off. At the time I was shocked and astounded as well as very ashamed at all the things I had ever done, said, or thought in my lifetime that were wrong. I was very grateful for knowing that the life review is real and for having the opportunity to change some things about myself while I am still alive in the physical.

In the reading we had just given, despite his recent departure, the spirit was able to come through and provide information about the circumstances of his choice, giving answers to some unresolved questions and some comfort to the sitter. When we give readings, we always discuss the latent abilities all people have for spirit communication, and attempt to assist the sitter in finding and developing their own method of communication with their deceased loved one if they wish to do so.

CONCLUSIONS

Based upon comments from the other side, research, reading, and personal analysis, I have drawn some of my own conclusions regarding the following topics.

Is there right and wrong?

Yes. That is why we come to earth – to learn right and wrong by experience.

Can we do wrong in the afterlife?

No. The environment does not permit harm to ourselves or others.

Do we know what is right and wrong instantly when we arrive in the afterlife?

No. That is why we have a life review, discussions with our guides, and those we interacted with in our earth lives.

Do we instantly become perfect as soon as we die?

No. Perfection is a process with learning over many earth incarnations and between earth lives in the afterlife.

What are spirit bodies? Are they real or just a thought or hallucination? What is reality?

Spirit bodies are not just a thought, a hallucination, but are not fixed or inflexible as they are in the more solid environment on earth. They have an actual substance, but not a fixed physical substance as on earth. They have a substance at a higher rate of vibration that is thought responsive and can be changed or altered in appearance.

Reality is more than the limited physical reality we know on earth and is accompanied by a greater spiritual reality. Reality is inclusive of both and most of us are not fully aware of the spiritual portion of reality when we are in the physical body.

Reality is what we see, feel, and perceive around us, and what we create within the limitations of our environment. Reality on the other side is said to be more diverse than the reality comprehended on earth by our five senses. When on earth, we only know our reality as the input from our senses or what we personally experience. On the other side it is reported that our experiences are limited only by our imagination with the universal stipulation that we not harm others. Spirits purportedly have greater powers of creation, greater faculties, greater knowledge, and more abundant potential.

How do spirits communicate with one another?

More directly by thought. Thought is transferred from one spirit to another in the form of images, feelings, concepts, awareness, sounds, ideas, and visions, directly without need for intervening physical apparatus and nervous systems.

Why do different mediums come to different conclusions about our reality and what is truth?

Because we are all limited in the human body and our understanding is created by different experiences. Subsequently, our mental interpretations and conclusions are different from one another. We each form our own ideas of what is the truth that are unique to us. Our own opinions, preferences, and personalities are reflected in everything we do, including in our mediumship readings. The communicating spirit has to overcome our mental prejudices and emotions and to give us theirs. Depending on how advanced the medium's abilities are, they may color or influence the message with their own feelings, opinions, and personalities. They must get their own "ego" out of the way to deliver a clear message.

Furthermore, we must first believe that something exists before we can attempt to explain it and pursue it. Then we must be open-minded enough to examine it without prejudice and attempt to explore that frontier without the predetermined mindset we have that applies to our physical existence. We must be willing to incorporate new ideas and possibilities into our "truth". At one time it was heresy to postulate that the earth was round, not flat, and that our sun wasn't the center of the universe. It takes courage and determination to explore a new reality, a new venue that may challenge the deeply held established beliefs.

What is love?

Individual love

Caring for another and another's welfare, not just the self; sharing life with another as companions and helpmates; uniting on a common path, forming a bond, and assisting one another in harmony and empathy; sharing experiences, activities, ideas, thoughts, feelings, interests, goals, and purpose; achieving spiritual and physical fulfillment together.

Humanitarian love

Respecting all life, not mistreating others, tolerating differences, interacting peacefully, practicing charity and helpfulness, acting in kindness and compassion.

Why do some authors writing about the afterlife say that we are all related, all one?

Just as we share a common genetic heritage when we are in the body, as souls we share a common origin from God or Source, making us all equal and related as souls in our origin, one big "soul family".

How is the afterlife different from earth life?

Uniqueness persists, but many limitations dissolve. Opportunities in variety of experience expand. Communication is facilitated. Negatives cannot be experienced as they are in a physical dimension. Love is more apparent. The roles necessary in human life such as mother, husband, child are not necessary or relevant. We can have and experience whatever we wish as long as we don't choose to harm others.

Why are we not clearly told about what the afterlife is truly like?

We are meant to come to earth to learn lessons without being consciously aware of our history, starting with a clean slate so to speak. Any previous lives or awareness of the afterlife is not meant to prejudice or influence our earth life choices and decisions. We are meant to make choices, express ourselves, and act upon our free will honestly, without outside influence and coercion. That is how we learn from our choices and decisions and change and improve our character. Not outside factors, only what we know and have learned in our hearts, should guide us.

We are learning and being tested without force. We learn by freedom of our own actions and their consequences. We would negate the learning experience, which requires free will, if we did not have freedom of action and choice.

If we knew that all of our actions and thoughts were being observed and recorded, we would not choose freely of our own volition, but we would instead artificially alter our choices to conform to expectations, rather than acting truthfully on the desires of our hearts. We wouldn't be able to act with honesty if we knew our thoughts were perceived and our actions observed. How many people speed when they know a police car is observing them? Would you want someone to be faithful to you because they are under 24 hour surveillance and are afraid to be caught or because they choose to be faithful on their own because they love you and don't want to hurt you? I believe that Source does not want people to act good because they are forced to or because of fear of punishment, but because they choose good in their hearts regardless of whether anyone else is watching or not.

If we knew for a fact that there is no death and that a finer, more wonderful afterlife awaited us, perhaps we wouldn't take this life seriously.

Not all knowledge and awareness can be given to us, because that would artificially affect our choices in our earth lives, by which we are learning and being judged. Also, we are all at different levels of development, and are only given knowledge that we are capable of understanding, processing, and utilizing at the level we are currently at.

Are all of our relationships with our guides the same?

No. Guides are spirits just as human beings are spirits in bodies. We establish different relationships as human beings. We also establish different relationships with other spirits after physical death. Likewise, we have different relationships with our guides.

Their general purpose is to help us navigate our earth lives and accomplish the lessons and learning we came to earth to experience. If they told us all the answers, we would never learn from our own experiences. As such, we interact differently. Part of that relationship is our agreed-upon expectations, needs, and contract, which are different for each individual and his or her guide.

The nature of life

We live in a universe that consists of good and bad, negative and positive. Source is good and with our gift of free will, we learn to act and express our free will in a manner consistent with goodness, kindness, and love.

We are in training. Our afterlife environment and experience will be in accordance with our judgment, desire, thought, and intention, and will match our level of spiritual development. We come to earth to test our thoughts in the cauldron of human experience and to learn.

PERSONAL LOVE – A FINAL THOUGHT

Is personal love tainted or inferior? No. Do we have to deny ourselves personal love to embrace a greater spiritual goal, a higher calling or purpose? No.

In the expression of selfless acts, of kindness compassion and charity, of benevolent deeds and philanthropic causes, one is not required to renounce personal companionship, to forgo individual ties.

Our greater cause does not exclude love. It is made from love. It is love.

It is simply a different manifestation within the rainbow that is love, which encompasses many different expressions, many different variations within the greater entirety, many rays of different colors and frequencies, all beautiful, all shining in the composite spectacle.

THE FINAL ASSESSMENT

The hardest part of any learning experience is putting what you know into practice. There are always prerequisites and you must do the groundwork in order to have the fundamentals at your disposal. But after you have gained the requisite knowledge, you must then apply it to real life situations.

Knowing can be easy, but performing difficult. Learning where the nerves, veins and arteries are, where the muscles attach, which bone is which, where the organs are and how they function, is requisite knowledge for a surgeon, but putting the scalpel to the skin and performing the operation is an entirely different matter. It requires a different set of skills – hand and eye coordination, knowing how to facilitate the order of events, cutting and suturing the tissues, knowing what to do in an emergency, all of the things that you can't learn just from books.

Although this is a very specific example, it can be applied as a template to most situations in life. In anything you hope to achieve, you must have the desire, will power, determination and intelligence to gain the needed knowledge and then to apply it in a practical situation. This is true for any job you perform, any task you undertake.

The question is what have you done with what you know? Have you used your knowledge well? Have you affected others' lives for the better? Have you successfully negotiated your own problems, troubles, and challenges in life? At the end of your life, when you face the ultimate question of mortality, will someone be able to say about you, "Well done, good and faithful servant?"

THE FINISHING TOUCH

Harvey's guide speaks regarding mediumship:

Trust the spirit within you to be a clear conduit from the spirit from above. A true communication is from spirit above, through the medium's spirit, to the spirit of the sitter.

My guide speaks regarding our life journeys:

Walk in truth. Make your life what it was meant to be. Keep your life in the hands of God. Don't be overcome by despair or others' insults. Maintain integrity. Keep your faith. Be close to the ones you love. Be truthful with yourself and others. There's only one person you can blame for anything that you have not accomplished and that is you. Keep moving forward. Don't be dismayed. Follow your heart .Don't lose hope. Make this your best journey ever. Don't lose love. That is the greatest gift you can ever have.

POSTSCRIPT

What is reality?

Reality as we know it is only what we experience through our senses. Sound and sight are not part of the firsthand reality of someone born blind or deaf. How many concepts put forth by scientific men in the past have proven false by investigation with more advanced instruments? Reality for us is what we can hear or see and we are limited by the capacity of our senses. Reality for a dog is something different, as they can hear sounds we can't.

We extend our conception of reality with instruments that can measure beyond what our bodily senses can detect. At any given time in history, our evolving definition of reality is only as good as the instruments we have at our disposal at that time.

It would be foolish for a man to say that what we perceive as reality at any given moment is all there is. If we sincerely believed that, there would be no need to expend our efforts in developing new instruments or conducting new experiments. Scientific development would be at a standstill.

I once had a teacher who was a medical doctor, and he said, at any given time, 50% of the absolutes we accept in medicine to be true are absolutely false. That is why we have progress. Reality is not evolving. We are, and our perception of reality is changing.

I had a professor of religion in college who said we all have faith whether we know it or not. He didn't mean faith in a God, but a broader faith. There was a time not so long ago before DNA analysis when we believed our parents were our biological parents, and most of us didn't attempt to prove it. Every day we make assumptions that are an exercise of faith. We make plans for the future – for jobs, marriage, education, homes, travel – but we don't really know whether or not we will die or be killed that afternoon. We believe the things friends and loved ones tell us. We espouse certain political or religious beliefs among the many civilization holds, without any proof that our convictions are "true". We in effect assume life is worth living when we seek to survive, eat, and find shelter. Every day we act on premises, values, principles, convictions, and assumptions we can't prove. These are all a matter of faith.

Everyone has these, even the most trenchant skeptic! Every time we exercise a choice we demonstrate faith. We couldn't act without it. Every time we embrace a belief we do so in faith. Some people think computers are good. Others think they are bad. Some people believe there is a God, while others believe there isn't. It takes just as much faith to believe there is one as to believe there isn't one, since none of us can prove it either way by scientific standards.

Furthermore, we trust what our senses are telling us. But how much don't we perceive? How much don't we know? We exercise judgments daily. Belief systems determine a great deal of how a country is run, what society accepts for rules, what behavior is good or bad, and individually we make choices and perform acts every day that are based upon preferences, beliefs, and faith. We all hold beliefs we cannot prove are right.

More and more, instruments are being developed that detect a "paranormal" reality we can't see or hear with our normal five senses. Remember that there was a long time before microscopes could see viruses, but now they can be detected. A skeptic in those earlier days would have said they didn't exist. How we would have been condemned at one time if we had said that something like iron wasn't really solid, but permeated by spaces and made up of tiny particles called atoms and electrons.

To believe wholesale and unquestioningly is as limited as to dismiss what we don't currently "know" or can't see unquestioningly. Those who deny the reality of the unseen unquestioningly are no different from those who believe anything unquestioningly. There is a middle road of questioning, speculation, and investigation. If we didn't entertain possibilities, we would never advance as a civilization.

At any level of development we see only a small piece of the puzzle. Those who have the intellectual curiosity to find out more are the engineers of our future, the ones to introduce and eventually prove new concepts, like those that former scientists were persecuted, imprisoned, and executed for — such as having the audacity to suggest the world might be round, not flat, or the earth or sun might not be the center of the universe.

Those who challenge our current conceptions of reality will always be a threat to some who have dearly held beliefs or a personal agenda. The beliefs of those who accept certain notions unquestioningly are no different from the beliefs of those who condemn any questioning or rigidly deny that there might be any greater reality than the small one which they can currently see with their limited tools. The most advanced tools we have now are as archaic as the ones we look at with amusement from the past. The horse and buggy have given way to the jet. Is that where we stop? It is just as ignorant to deny any reality other than the small one available to your present level of knowledge as it is to accept that a premise is real without questioning, pursuing, and seeking.

Should we believe without question or disbelieve without question? No. They are the same. We should question, seek, conjecture, experiment, and learn. Only in our creative endeavors do our dreams and conjectures transform into reality.

In short, all of us have faith, even the most "dyed in the wool" skeptic. It is just as uninformed to definitively say that something doesn't or can't exist as it is to say unequivocally that something we can't prove does exist. Only those who walk out on a limb and are willing to look at something new expand our understanding of reality.

Most of what I discuss in this book is not based on proven scientific fact, but based on my own personal experiences. Many of us do not believe in something until it happens to us, and understandably so. I have had enough substantiation in my individual experiences to accept many currently inexplicable events as part of my individual reality. Each of us must find his or her own. Although something we experience may not warrant concrete proof for the public, it may justify our own reasonable belief, much like circumstantial evidence. As Proverbs states, "As a man thinketh, so he is." As Shakespeare said in "Hamlet", "There are more things in heaven and earth, Horatio, than are dreamt of in your philosophy."

May we find meaning and fulfillment in our lives. May we reach our greatest potential. May we be a blessing to others. May we find inner strength, joy, and peace in our hearts.

BIBLIOGRAPHY

Bethards, Betty, *There Is No Death*, (Petaluma, California: New Century, 2007) (Original Work Published 1977)

Borgia, Anthony, *Life in the World Unseen*, (Kindle Edition, 2009) (Original Work Published 1954)

Brown, Robert, *We Are Eternal*, (New York: Warner Books, 2003)

Cummins, Geraldine, *The Road to Immortality*, (Norfolk, England: Thetford, 1984) (Original Work Published 1932)

Cummins, Geraldine, *Beyond Human Personality*, (London, England: Psychic Press, 1935)

Cummins, Geraldine, *Travelers in Eternity*, (London, England: Knapp, Drewett & Sons, 1948)

Dresser, Charlotte & Rafferty, Fred, *Life Here and Hereafter*, (San Jose, California: Cosmos, 1927)

Dresser, Charlotte & Rafferty, Fred, *Spirit World and Spirit Life*, (Kindle Edition, 2010) (Original Work Published 1922)

Eaton, Barry, *Afterlife*, (Crows Nest NSW, Australia: Allen & Unwin, 2011)

Flint, Leslie, *Afterlife Communication, Library of Leslie Flint Seances*, (adcguides.com/librarynames.htm)

Hamilton-Parker, Craig, *What to Do When You Are Dead*, (New York, New York: Sterling Publishing Company, 2010)

Kelway-Bamber, Claude H., *Claude's Book*, (New York, New York: Henry Holt and Company, 1919)

Kelway-Bamber, L., *Claude's Second Book*, (Whitefish, Montana: Kessinger, 2010) (Original Work Published 1920)

Kruickshank, Kelvin, *Bridging the Gap*, (Rosedale, North Shore, New Zealand: Penguin Books, 2010)

Kruickshank, Kelvin, *Finding the Path,* (Rosedale, North Shore, New Zealand: Penguin Books)

Kruickshank, Kelvin, *Inside the Medium,* (Rosedale, North Shore, New Zealand: Penguin Books, 2013)

Kruickshank, Kelvin, *Taking the Journey,* (Rosedale, North Shore, New Zealand: Penguin Books, 2015)

Kruickshank, Kelvin, *Walking in Light*, (Rosedale, North Shore, New Zealand: Penguin Books, 2009)

Lodge, Oliver, & Lodge, Raymond, *Raymond or Life and Death, Vol. I and II*, (Kindle Edition, 2011) (Original Work Published 1916)

Marks, Jeffrey A., *The Afterlife Interviews*, Vol. I and II, (Mukitleo, Washington: Arago Press, 2013 and 2014)

Russo, Kim, *The Happy Medium*, (New York, New York: HarperCollins Publishers, Inc., 2016)

Sandys, Cynthia, *The Awakening Letters,* (Channel Islands, Great Britain: Neville Spearman Limited, 1978)

Sandys, Cynthia, *The Awakening Letters, Vol. II,* (Essex, England: The C. W. Daniel Company Limited, 1986)

Scott, John, *As One Ghost to Another*, (London, England: Spiritualist Press, 1948)

Sculthorpe, Frederick C., *Excursions to the Spirit World*, (London, England: The Greater World Association, 1961)

Spurgin, Nora M., *Insights into the Afterlife*, (New York, New York, Women's Federation for World Peace)

St. Clair, Shanna Spalding, *Karma I and II, (no location provided: S. C. Walter, 1993)*

Swain, Jasper, *On the Death of My Son*, (Northhamptonshire, England: The Aquarian Press, 1974)

Swedenborg, Emanuel, *The Delights of Wisdom Pertaining to Conjugal Love*, (Kindle Edition, original work published, 1850)

Winninger, Toni Ann, *Life Lessons*, (Lake Bluff, Illinois: Celestial Voices, 2012)

Winninger, Toni Ann, *Talking with Leaders of the Past*, (Lake Bluff, Illinois: Celestial Voices, 2008)

Winninger, Toni Ann, *Talking with Twentieth Century Men,* (Lake Bluff, Illinois: Celestial Voices, 2008)

Vogel, Gretchen, *Choices in the Afterlife*, (Keene, New Hampshire: Choices Publishing, 2010)

ABOUT THE AUTHOR

Prudence Ann Smith, MD, FACR, is a physician and a fellow of the American College of Radiology. Dr. Smith received her education from Northwestern University, the University of Illinois, the University of Minnesota, the University of Wisconsin, and Jefferson Medical College.

Dr. Smith had a grandmother who was a medium, and this background, combined with Smith's unique experience in the scientific disciplines, helps her analyze life's deepest spiritual questions in a truly unique way.

Dr. Smith's other books include *The Afterlife*, *Two Mediums*, *Making Rainbows*, *Poems from the Heart*, and *My Life in Poetry: Volumes I and II*.

Answers from the Afterlife was written with contributions by Harvey Paul Karr.

www.ingramcontent.com/pod-product-compliance
Lightning Source LLC
LaVergne TN
LVHW051038080426
835508LV00019B/1576